BREAKING INTO SONG

Essays, Articles and Interviews
On Musical Theatre
By Mel Atkey

Friendlysong Books
Vancouver ⊙ London

Published by The Friendlysong Company, Inc.
4827 Georgia Street, Delta, British Columbia, Canada
V4K 2T1

Cataloguing:

    Atkey, Mel (1958-)

    Breaking Into Song – Essays, Articles and
    Interviews on Musical Theatre
    ISBN 978-0-9916957-3-7

    1 – Musicals – International – History and
    criticism.

Table of Contents

Preface:
Uncool (And Proudly So)

I have discovered a writer whom I believe may be my opposite number. Not that we are actually opponents, but we approach musical theatre from opposite perspectives.

Dave Malloy is an OBIE award-winning Brooklyn-based composer, performer and sound designer. He also happens to write what some people call musicals. I am a Vancouver-born, London-based composer, lyricist, author and occasional lecturer. I also happen to write musicals. The difference is he's embarrassed to admit it, whereas I shout it from the rooftops at every opportunity.

In a 2011 blog, Malloy explained, "while I love music, and I love theater, I am acutely aware of the stigma of the term 'musical theater,' of all it has come to connote and the kneejerk reactions the genre tends to elicit. My community is largely one of experimental, downtown theater artists and musicians, for whom the love of musicals is either nonexistent, highly qualified, or a shameful secret." [1]

My background is different. My community is not the avant-garde downtown artists and musicians, it is those whom Malloy calls "musical theatre geeks",

---

[1] http://howlround.com/a-slushy-in-the-face-musical-theater-music-and-the-uncool accessed 24 June 2014.

those who live and breathe musicals, much like *The Drowsy Chaperone*'s 'Man-in-Chair'. And just in case you want to jump to one of those knee-jerk conclusions, I am a heterosexual middle class WASP male who doesn't fit easily into any of the ghetto-like pockets that critics want to deposit me in.

Malloy says, "The reason so much musical theater sounds bad and 'uncool' to so many ears, particularly when it flirts with rock, is because it lacks authenticity. Because it is being sung by people who aren't rock singers. They are acting. It's an obvious but critical fact; actors perform in fundamentally different ways from musicians." Of course they do. When Olivier played Hamlet, people expected to see an interpretation of Hamlet, not the histrionics of an actor. It's true that in the audience may be some of what Canadian musical writer John MacLachlan Gray calls "cultural souvenir hunters", but Olivier's responsibility to the audience was to present a representation of Shakespeare's character, not a manifestation of his own persona. Rock music cherishes "rawness" whereas musical theatre requires discipline.

Is being "cool" even good? Or does it make your work ephemeral, like last year's trends? When I was a teenager, I was decidedly "un-cool". I learned – painfully – not to trust those voices that urged me to follow the crowd. It always amuses me when those who claim to be at the cutting edge concern themselves with whether or not they are cool. Then again, the "cutting edge" has always, to me, denoted something to protect my fingers from. What I care about is learning a craft and doing it well. So, you see, I understand "un-cool". I get it. I embrace it. I own it.

That said, when it came to learning my craft, I took an unusual path to get there. When I was in high school, I didn't get the leading roles in the school musicals. Having the voice of a tone-deaf hyena and the physique of an arthritic coat-rack didn't help. The drama teacher strongly resented any implications that she had played favourites in the casting of school plays, so I decided that rather than argue with her, I would just go my own way. With a group of fellow misfits, we formed our own group, hired a local auditorium and put on our own show – a musical comedy version of Shakespeare's "Scottish play", *Macdeath*. The school authorities threw every obstacle at their disposal in our path.

With a level of wit that remains unsurpassed, composer Mark Telford and I penned songs like "Coffee for Three":

> When I was a younger girl
> and didn't know how life would turn
> I used to sit by the fire
> and watch the bark-mulch burn.

(Well, at least it is a proper rhyme.)

And then there was "The Baseball Song". This deathless aria was sung by Macbeth and Banquo to the three witches (as a diversionary tactic – don't ask). Pulsating with confidence that I was the next Mel Brooks, I sent the script to Gareth Wigan, vice-president of Twentieth Century Fox (and husband of *Oliver*'s Georgia Brown). He replied: "At the risk of sounding pompous, I'm afraid I found nothing in it to recommend it..."

But it appears that I was to have the last laugh. While doing an internet search of my name a few years ago, I came across a site called "A List of Baseball Songs Identified at the Library of Congress". Number 67 was "The Baseball Song" by Mark Telford and Louis [Melville] Atkey. This was all contained in a book of baseball trivia called *Everything Baseball*[2]. As best as I can figure, somebody trawled the copyright registrations and uncovered this gem. How anybody stupid enough to conceive such a project could muster the acumen to carry out the research is

---

[2] James Mote, *Everything Baseball*, Prentice Hall, New York, 1989

beyond me, but there you have it. It is not possible to be more trivial than that.[3]

We pulled it off – sort of. I can't honestly say that there were any predictions of great things for the talent on display – although in fact our leading actor Michael Robinson would turn professional and pass on his improv skills to other actors, including Cate Blanchett. The only other legacy is the opening number "I'd Like to Get Friendly With You", sung by the witches to Macbeth and Banquo, which gave The Friendlysong Company its name.

After high school, I did not take the conventional route of going to university, as nobody had yet had the inspiration/courage to attempt to teach musical theatre at the academic level. Instead, I set my own course of study. My first stage was to join the University of British Columbia's Musical Theatre Society. (Not being a UBC student was not a barrier to this – some of my colleagues included future *Stargate* actress Teryl Rothery and *Flesh and Bone* creator Moira Walley-Beckett, neither of whom were students.) We were led by veteran choreographer Grace Macdonald, whose students included dancer Jeff Hyslop. Mussoc was where I learned to truly love the form.

My next step was a brief career as an arts journalist on radio, TV and in print. The television aspect was particularly short-lived, as my face had all the expressiveness of a stagnant cess pool. I did,

---

[3] Yes it is – they left out the subtitle, "No, It's Not Cricket".)

however, manage to see around two hundred shows a year, including the Broadway touring companies that came to nearby Seattle. I also managed, during this time, to do a number of celebrity interviews, two of which are included in this anthology.

For two years – from 1981-83 – I wrote theatre reviews for CHQM-FM and for the *Georgia Straight* newspaper, while also contributing occasional articles to *Playboard* (roughly Vancouver's equivalent to *Playbill*), two of which are also included here.

In 1983 I left Vancouver for Toronto, where for a short time I was a member of the Guild of Canadian Musical Theatre Writers' Lehman Engel workshops. I thought I was going to be a big fish in a small pond, and rise quickly to the top. I learned two things:

> a) I was a small fish in a big pond, and
> b) A fish rising to the top is not a good omen.

I struggled for a few years – nearly had a show produced starring James Doohan, *Star Trek*'s "Scotty" – until I came under the influence of noted television producer Norman Campbell, composer of *Anne of Green Gables – The Musical*. He got me started on the next phase of my education – the study of my own musical theatre heritage. This eventually became my book *Broadway North – The Dream of a Canadian Musical Theatre* and its later follow-up, *A Million Miles from Broadway – Musical Theatre Beyond New York and London*.

Then in 1991 I moved to London, where I became a Professional Writer Associate of Mercury Musical Developments and met the American director and writer Bob Sickinger, with whom I would write two musicals. I also began to lecture on musical theatre after attending a conference where I met a professor who taught a course in Canada based on my book *Broadway North*. Deciding that any students on such a course deserved to hear it straight from the horse's mouth, I finally took the first steps toward earning my MA in Musical Theatre (yes, Virginia, there now is such a thing) at Goldsmiths University of London.

The following is my approach toward "scholarly" research: if it looks like a duck, has feathers and quacks, then it's quite probably a duck. Nevertheless, in academic circles you must also sample the duck's DNA. You should be cautioned that, in practical fact, the attempt to extract it may result in your being attacked by a razor-sharp bill. Thus it is suggested to all but the most pedantic that it is indeed a duck.

So, it may be un-cool. It may not please all of the academics. But, in any case, what follows is some of the fruitage of my thirty-five year learning curve.

Stephen Schwartz: Extraordinary

My first exposure to the musicals of Stephen Schwartz was in 1973 when I attended a screening of the film version of *Godspell*. In front of me were a group of nuns who literally howled with laughter throughout the comically role-played parables. I saw it on stage for the first time a few months later in a production at Ford's Theatre in Washington, D.C. I was just fifteen years old, and this had a marked influence on me.

Stephen Schwartz: Extraordinary.

In the early seventies, he was Broadway's wizkid. By the time he was twenty-five, he had composed the music for two hit musicals, 'Godspell' and 'Pippin'. Now he is the subject of a new sixty minute stereo radio special.

CREATIVE VARIETY RADIO
WORTH WATCHING

Friendlysong Radio
Productions. Inc. Syndicate

BOX 134. DELTA. B C. V4K 3N8 .(604) 948-2664

In the early 1970s, Stephen Schwartz had three hit shows running simultaneously in New York – in addition to *Godspell*, there was also *Pippin* and *The Magic Show*. Throughout my teen years, he and Andrew Lloyd Webber were my favourite composers. The latter would ultimately fall from this lofty perch, but Stephen Schwartz remains as a role model to many on both a professional and personal level.

My first actual contact with him came in 1980 when, at the age of 22, I produced a syndicated radio series called *Broadway Melodies*. Record producer Bruce

Yeko, who had released the original cast recording of *The Baker's Wife* on his Original Cast Records label, put me in touch with him.

Vancouver's Arts Club Theatre had just presented a production of *Pippin* starring Jeff Hyslop, who had once been considered for the part in the original New York production.

I was a novice both to musical theatre and to radio. With the budget of a frayed, second-hand shoestring, I did the interview via telephone – me in Vancouver, Stephen at his home in Ridgefield, Connecticut. I hatched the idea of running tape recorders at both ends of the conversation. He would then mail me the tape of his end of the conversation. (Since his tape recorder was "on the fritz", he borrowed a cassette from his then-infant son Scott, now a Broadway director.)

I had never done any sort of celebrity interview before, and my knowledge of musical theatre was certainly not what it is today. I gathered questions from other theatre people I knew. I even went to a rehearsal of a local community *Godspell* production and recorded questions from two of its cast members: one of them, Bruce Dow, would end up becoming a leading musical theatre actor, director and educator in Canada, a twelve year veteran of the Stratford Festival who eventually made his Broadway debut in *Jane Eyre*, co-directed by none other than Scott Schwartz – the same one who loaned his tape recorder. (The other cast member, Wendy Long, became a journalist for a leading Vancouver newspaper.)

My questions were often frankly naïve and trite ("Which comes first, music or lyrics?" etc.) but his answers were always insightful. Now, it's interesting as a historical snapshot. This was before his career revival, following the initial failures of *the Baker's Wife*, *Working* and, later, *Rags* and *Children of Eden* (all of which were later successfully revived). The triumphs of *Prince of Egypt*, *Pocahontas*, *Enchanted* and, especially *Wicked* were a long way off, and he was seriously questioning whether he would ever write another musical.

This is the complete and unexpurgated interview, of which selections were used in the 1980 episode of *Broadway Melodies* called "Stephen Schwartz: Extraordinary".

Bruce Dow: How much musical training have you had? And where?

Stephen Schwartz: Well, let's see. I took piano lessons from about the time I was in second grade. Then I went to Julliard, which is a rather well-known music school. When I was in high school they had a preparatory division there and I took piano and composition and a lot of theory there, etc.

BD: For someone who is interested in getting started, where did you start to go?

SS: The best way to pursue a career as a musical theatre composer, it seems to me, is to write musicals and attempt to get them done, get them produced, once you have done a show that you feel good about. Obviously if you are a composer and don't do your own lyrics, that means finding a lyricist. If you are a composer-lyricist, that means find a script writer, or adapting a script yourself. But I have found, and most people I know who have gotten into this business have found that if you start out that way, even if you have to make some compromises along the way in terms of what script you use, sooner or later somebody hears about you or you hook up with somebody or other and it goes from there. You sort of then learn the rules as you go along. There seems to be no specific formula: it's not the kind of thing where you say go to such and such a place at such and such a time then wait. You have to just get started.

BD: Were you the originator of the idea for *Godspell* and why did you pick a religious theme? If so, why did you think it would be successful? Just for the religious reasons?

SS: No, I was not the originator of the idea for *Godspell*. The idea for *Godspell* was generated by John-Michael Tebelak who adapted the material and also directed the original production. He was a young man who for a while had been considering becoming an Episcopal priest – or minister, I'm not exactly sure of the correct term. So he had several years of thinking in those lines which really reflected his own feelings that the church had lost the joy and the wonder and the humour that he felt was in it at the beginning and he felt that it had become very, very solemn and over-burdened with ceremony, and this was his attempt to go back to some of what he felt was some of the original joy that could be found in the religion. My having to do with it was mainly that the producers of the show who saw it as a sort-of non-musical at the Café LaMama which is an experimental theatre in New York City were then interested in making it into a full-fledged musical and moving it to Off-Broadway at which point they called me and I went down to see it and was very, very intrigued with the idea and then wrote the score. I can claim absolutely no credit for the conception.

BD: How many musicals did you write before you got the first one produced or the first one was a success and do you think you'd ever go back to those ideas and try them again?

SS: Well, I did – let's see. I used to do a musical every year at college. I went to what is now Carnegie-Mellon and at that time was Carnegie Tech in Pittsburgh, Pennsylvania. They had an organisation called Scotch 'n' Soda which was an extra-curricular organisation that put on a musical show every year. I wrote the show the four years that I was there. The third one in my junior year was *Pippin*[4], and that's

---

[4] At Carnegie, it was called *Pippin, Pippin* with a book by Ron Strauss. Schwartz was credited as "Lawrence Stephens", a play on his first and

what I came to New York with trying to sell. Of course that got on, and before *Pippin* got produced I was asked to do *Godspell*. I don't really have too many shows in my trunk. Of the other shows I did at college, I really don't feel the ideas really have enough merit to pursue. But I was one of the fortunate ones that was not trundling several shows around trying to get them produced. Basically everything that I have done that I have felt I wanted to have produced did get produced. It wasn't always successful, but at least it got on.

Wendy Long: One thing I'd like to ask is that *Godspell* is rather a unique sort of production in that all the characters stay on the stage the whole time. I'm just wondering, did you pattern this play after any other plas – for example *The Fantasticks* is similar in that it has a small cast and they all seem to be on stage for the whole time.

SS: I do know that it was not patterned in any way after any other show. I haven't seen *The Fantasticks* for about ten years or fifteen years or so, but my recollection of it is that the cast is in fact not on that stage for the whole time. What John-Michael was after was to get a kind of ensemble feeling and a group energy and if there were entrances and exits made that would have been difficult. Also, he not only wouldn't let people make entrances and exits, he put a cyclone fence around the stage so it was clear that there was no way off the stage, and in fact

---

second names, Stephen Lawrence. None of the book nor score of this version survived into the Broadway incarnation.

people entered the stage by coming through the audience, so that was really part of his original conception. There's a kind of group energy generated by actors when they're on the stage all the time. In *Working*, though we weren't able to do this for some technical reasons in the New York production, I always like to have the entire cast on the stage the entire time, watching the other monologues if they're not directly involved themselves.

WL: I've noticed that most of the songs in *Godspell* are actually adapted from old hymns. For example, "Turn Back, O Man" is a nice little hymn, and you've turned it into something pretty raunchy. How did you decide on that and how did you go about doing that? It's a very unique idea, especially when people sit down , they see the song "Turn Back O Man", they go "yes, I know that hymn" , and then it comes out complete raunch. How did you decide on that? It's wonderful.

SS: I'll answer the specific part of the question first. "Turn Back O Man", the girl performing that section, the girl we decided was going to do that hymn in the show, Sonia Manzano was playing a sort-of raunchy character. Her character dictated the tone of the song. Generally, I think that's what happened. In the case of "Day By Day", we were trying to make a very simple and sincere statement, so that dictated the simplicity of that song. "All Good Gifts" is a bit more passionate. "Bless the Lord" is a celebration , so that dictated what happened musically with that. Basically, there's an emotion you want to express or a character, and I viewed the songs in *Godspell* as being really no different from any other show tune except that the lyrics were not expressing the emotion so much, so it had to be done purely with music and the sub-text, and let the lyrics carry it that way. Obviously we couldn't do something that was completely inappropriate to the lyric but I felt that there were choices about how to interpret the lyric based upon where it was coming in the show and which character was singing it.

Mel Atkey: What was the first show you were ever involved in?

SS: The first professional show that I was every involved in was *Butterflies Are Free*[5] for which I contributed the title song and had very, very little to do with anything else. Like most people, I had a great deal of semi-professional and summer-stock experience and before that high school experience and before that grade school experience, so I'm not exactly sure where to start answering that question.

MA: Did you perform on stage before you started writing?

SS: Yeah, in summer stock I did a couple of things, and of course also when I went to college, since Carnegie-Tech was essentially a drama school. It's really not my favourite thing to do. I have friends who are actors and they get a great deal of pleasure out of doing the same thing over and over again and

[5] By Leonard Gershe, opened 21 October 1969, Booth Theatre

attempting to refine it or attempting to see if they can recapture a performance, etc. That's not what interests me. I tend to have a goal in mind and want to achieve it and once it's achieved I'm really not interested in repeating it. You see, if I were an actor and let's say I was in a show for, whatever, four months, and at the end of the fourth month on one Saturday night I gave a performance that I felt, gee, that's the best I can do in this role, I'd just want to leave the show the next day. If you're a writer you just keep working on something and working on something until it's the best you know how to make it and then you say, "that's it, that's the best I can do" and move on to the next thing. It really has to do with what kind of thing interests you and where your "aesthetic personality" I guess is the term for it lies.

MA: Were you happy with the film version of *Godspell*?

SS: No, I have some problems with the film version. I feel that the basic tone was wrong. I think that the director [David Greene] who is a very gifted director and has done some very good work in other things – he did some of *Roots* and he did a thing called *The People Next Door* which I think was just wonderful – but for some reason I don't think he really understood *Godspell* and he sort-of got it confused with, perhaps *[Jesus Christ] Superstar* and with more prosaic concepts of the passion etc., and so he sort-of injected a sort of "Greatest Story Ever Told" aspect into it. I thought the character of Jesus was not at all what it had been conceived to be in the show *Godspell* and I thought that hurt the film.[6]

MA: How historically accurate is *Pippin*?

SS: Oh, not at all! Charlemagne did have an eldest son named Pepin who was in fact a hunchback , and who did participate in a plot to overthrow his father which was foiled, and Charlemagne did have a wife named Fastrada who was rather scheming. Other than that really, beyond the names of the characters and their relationship to each other there's virtually no historical accuracy at all.

MA: Does the story have anything to do with the novel *Pepin*?[7]

SS: Nothing whatsoever.

MA: How much was the show changed from its original concept by Bob Fosse?

SS: Quite a good deal, I would say. The thing about *Pippin* is the show changed a great deal even before it got to Bob as it went through its journey trying to get it onto Broadway because the thing about doing a show where you're in a sort-of never-neverland time and you have characters who only are relationships and don't really have their own story to tell, the thing is you can impose almost anything on them. Bob had

---

[6] He later told me that if the entire film had been up to the standard of the "All For the Best" sequence, he would have been happy.

[7] *Episodes from Pepin and Charlemagne* by Alexandre Dumas

some feelings of his own and some things he was trying to deal with and I feel that he imposed them on the show for whatever it was worth, better or worse.[8]

MA: Who initiated the idea?

SS: The idea initiated with me in college, and then when I came to New York some people who had heard a cast recording of the college production indicated some interest in it so I began to pursue it.

MA: Which part, Pippin or the Leading Player was to have the main focus?

SS: There was no Leading Player until Ben Vereen auditioned for us, so obviously it originated with Pippin and when we found Ben the show was restructured so that several small parts were combined and put into the character of the Leading Player.

MA: Was it intended to be a big production?

SS: Once Bob came into it, it was certainly intended to. I mean, Bob 's concept was what you saw on the stage and I don't think he changed his intention.

---

[8] John Rubinstein said, "Stephen was genuinely concerned that his work was being turned into a vaudeville. Bobby was just as genuinely concerned that this sentimental thing was going to have no guts. I thought they were both right." Cited in Martin Gottfried, *All His Jazz – The Life and Death of Bob Fosse* , Da Capo Press, New York, 1990, p.252

MA: The reason why I ask this is that the Arts Club[9] production was a very scaled-down version and sometimes the way it came off it almost looked like that was what it had been designed for.

SS: Well, I think Bob's production was what he meant it to be. It may not have been what I meant it to be but, you know, it is what it is. The show *Pippin* is a case where the director-choreographer had a very strong concept and also a very strong personality, and so it really became his work. It's difficult for me to answer too many questions about it because it was really out of my hands in many aspects.

MA: Was it originally intended to use a full orchestra?

SS: Yeah, I feel we were always talking about an orchestra, although I wasn't particularly happy with all the orchestrations[10]. It's hard for me to remember back that far, quite frankly. That's eight years ago. It was not a very happy working experience for me, and so I don't tend to dwell on it when I think about it. It's just very hard now trying to go back and remember what was in my mind at what time. I feel the show *Pippin* is over, it was very successful, it keeps being done and done, people like it very much, and that's enough for me. I don't tend to hold on to that experience.

---

[9] Arts Club Theatre, Vancouver, Britsih Columbia, 1980 Directed by Bill Millerd with Jeff Hyslop as Pippin and Kimble Hall as the Leading Player.
[10] The orchestrations were by Ralph Burns

MA: Do you remember if there were any songs written for it that were not used?

SS: Well, there were thousands! That's not literal, but there were several songs written as it went along its incarnation . But from the time we had what we felt was the final version to the time we opened, I think we eliminated one song and replaced two with two new songs in virtually the same spot.

MA: Which were the new songs?

SS: "Extraordinary" replaced a song called "Marking Time" and "Love Song" replaced a song called "Just Between the Two of Us". The "Love Song" replacement had to do with the cast[11] not really sounding very good doing the original song and so I tried to find a song that they would be able to sing better. And "Extraordinary" had to do with the fact that "Marking Time" didn't seem to work theatrically. It was the kind of song where the lyric was a little difficult to follow theatrically so we came up with something that was a little simpler.

MA: Do you feel there were any references in *All That Jazz* to *Pippin*?

SS: I don't know. I didn't see *All That Jazz*.

MA: There's a sequence in it called "Air-otica" that to me looked a lot like "The Flesh".

---

[11] John Rubinstein as Pippin, Jill Clayburgh as Catherine.

SS: It's possible. I mean, Bob has his motifs which he repeats because they're of concern to him and he's a very, very personal director and choreographer so I wouldn't be surprised, but I really can't comment on the film because I didn't see it.

MA: Was "With You" intended for its present context?

SS: No, not at all. I don't feel it really works in that context, and if I hadn't liked the song so much I probably would have cut it.

MA: What sort of context was it supposed to be?

SS: Well, it was supposed to be dine much straighter, and also to one girl.

MA: What do you think of the book for *Pippin* in its final version?

SS: I have a lot of reservations about it. I felt the book was stronger going in than it was coming out.

MA: Did you start to work with it alone or did you begin with Roger Hirson?

SS: Roger and I worked together for quite a while on it. Obviously when I did it in college I didn't do it with Roger Hirson, but then when we really began to pursue it as a possible New York production, Roger came into it. He was with it for a couple of years.

MA: Which do you begin with, music or lyrics?

SS: I think I begin with – especially if I'm writing for a show, I begin with the place I feel demands a number. You just have a feeling: "I need music here. I hear a song here, or I hear a musical number here". That will probably suggest a title and a sort of musical feel, and maybe a couple of lines of lyrics. Then I usually like to try to get as many of the lyrics done before I do music as possible because it's so much easier to do music than lyrics. It's much, much easier to fit music to lyrics than the other way around, but unfortunately music happens so much faster than lyrics that generally what happens is, I'll have maybe a chorus, or a verse or I'll have a little bit and I'll just say, "Well, maybe I'll go and see if I can set this just to see what it sounds like," and suddenly I have a whole song of music and once again and I end up having to spen two weeks filling in the lyrics.

MA: Have you ever worked with other lyricists?

SS: When I'm doing pop songs I always work with another lyricist because I'm not a very good pop lyricist. For shows, I generally do my own lyrics simply because I haven't really found anybody who I feel writes show lyrics that I feel work for me. Also, with a show I have very specific things that I want to say, usually dramatically, and I don't really like to give that up. But in pop lyrics, in general I almost never write pop songs on my own. Generally someone will send me a lyric and I'll set that if I like it.

MA: Can you give me some examples of pop songs that you've written that way?

SS: Let's see, what's fairly recent – oh, the new Jane Olivor album has a song called "Manchild Lullaby"[12] on it, and that's one of them.

MA: Who were your main teachers or influences?

SS: I'm often asked that question. I think it's very hard to answer because of course you're never fully aware. I know who I like and who I listen to and I suppose one is always influenced by that. A couple of days ago I was up in Toronto working on *The Magic Show* movie and the orchestrator[13] came in – I was showing him some stuff and he said, "Do you listen to Aaron Copland a lot?" and I said, "Why, yes, I do!" so obviously that showed up somewhere. He heard something that was Coplandesque. All I can answer is, classically, composers that I listen to or that I like very much are Copland and, oh, going back in time, Puccini, Mozart, Bach I guess are the ones that I enjoy listening to the most. Pop – it really varies. For a long time there are some people that I've liked. I almost always like everything James Taylor does. I like most of Paul Simon's work very, very much. Until the last couple of albums I was a rabid Joni Mitchell fan. I think I was influenced by Laura Nero.

---

[12] Lyrics by Leida Snow, from the album "The Best Side of Goodbye"
[13] Eric Robertson

These are recent but really I think the influences go back further for me when I was younger. The early Motown stuff, the early Supremes and Temptations, stuff like that. Folk stuff like The Weavers and that whole kind of late-fifties folk explosion. Those are things I like and tend to still remember, but where that shows up in my own music I really don't have any idea.

MA: To what degree do you feel that your own philosophies are expressed in each show?

SS: In a how? Very, very much. I mean, I always think everything one writes is autobiographical. I think it's pretty clear in a show like *Pippin* or even in the songs for *The Baker's Wife*, I think though I was writing for character, they really reflect emotions that in all cases are things I've felt. I think that's one of the reasons I sort of enjoyed doing the songs for *Baker's Wife* because it was like a little Freudian therapy session. But I think that anybody would tell you that, that they feel their work is...

MA: Do you mean specifically songs like "Gifts of Love"?

SS: Oh, yeah, I think all of them express sides of one's character and emotions that I have felt and situations I felt I had been in.

MA: Do you identify yourself then with the character of Pippin?

SS: Oh sure. Oh yeah. I mean, Roger and I used to always joke because I would identify with Pippin and he would identify with Charlemagne.

MA: How do you prepare the score for a show? To what point do you develop the music before it is turned over to an arranger?

SS: Very, very completely. By the time it goes to an arranger, it's really set, and I usually have very specific ideas about the arrangement which I will convey to the orchestrator. It's almost cemented in by the time the orchestrator gets it.

MA: Do you write it as a piano score?

SS: It depends on the song. If I feel the piano part or the orchestral accompaniment is important enough, then I'll write a complete part out. Sometimes I'll write out a complete part and then I'll write out some orchestral counter-melody lines that I want to hear. On the other hand there's some songs where all I'll give him is a lead sheet because I feel that the orchestral part is so obvious that – or it's not really about a lot of interesting little lines or about a rather intricate orchestral figure. If I feel it's a guitar song or a rhythm song or something it's foolish for me to write out a piano part. So it really depends on the song.

MA: Could you give us an example of a song for which you've just written lead sheets?

SS: Oh, sure. "I Guess I'll Miss the Man" from *Pippin* and "Simple Joys" from *Pippin* were both guitar songs so I just gave the orchestrator lead sheets and then talked about what I wanted. On the other hand a song like – since you asked about *Pippin*, I'll stick with that – a song like "Corner of the Sky" which has an extremely intricate piano part, I wrote the piano part out completely and then wrote stuff up above it, as well as obviously the vocal line.

MA: I understand that you're now working on the film version of *The Magic Show*.[14] Are you making any additions to the score?

SS: Oh, God, I'm making a lot of additions! It's really nice. It's like getting a second chance. There are four new songs in it and the lyrics to one of the songs have been rewritten substantially enough for me to really feel it qualifies almost as a new song. And obviously I cut a lot of material.

MA: What's the one being rewritten?

SS: "Style" has new lyrics which I feel are much better. It's the same content, I just feel that the jokes are better and the references are better.

MA: Which numbers are you cutting?

SS: I replaced "Solid Silver Platform Shoes" with a song called "It's Going to Take a Magician". I replaced a song called "A Bit of Villainy" which is not

[14] Directed by Norman Campbell,

on the album with what I think is a good song called "a Round for the Bad Guys". I replaced Charmin's song with another song. I replaced "West End Avenue" with a song called "Where Did the Magic Go?" and we cut a couple of songs.

MA: Charmin's song? Is that "Lion Tamer"?

SS: No. Oh, no. I wouldn't touch "Lion Tamer".[15] Charmin's song is called, in fact, "Charmin's Lament".

MA: Will the book be staying fairly close to the original?

SS: No, there's a new writer on it, a guy named Jerry Ross, but it's the original story. The same story line. It's just been tightened, and one hopes improved.

MA: *The Baker's Wife* had what many people believe to be your best score, yet it closed in the tryouts.[16] What went wrong?

---

[15] But CBC Television did. When *The Magic Show* was finally shown on TV in Canada in 1983 after failing to get a cinema release, the network went to a commercial just as the song was starting. Director Norman Campbell, an Emmy-winning CBC stalwart, stared at his TV screen in disbelief and disgust. It was eventually released on DVD with the song intact.

[16] Book by Joseph Stein and produced by David Merrick, based on the film *La Femme du Boulanger* directed by Marcel Pagnol and written by Pagnol and Jean Giono, It toured the US for six months in 1976 until the authors pulled the plug on it following its run at the Kennedy Centre.

SS: Oh, I think there were a lot of things wrong with the production. The casting was abominable.[17] There were many, many things wrong with the whole production, the whole look of the production. *The Baker's Wife* has been done recently in a couple of places with a revised book and on a whole kind-of smaller production scale and it's been done extremely successfully, so it looks like there's some real life in that project yet. One thing I learned, I must say, from those smaller productions is that it's a very small show, and if you take it too big, you just lose it totally.

MA: When you say a small show, do you mean a small orchestra?

SS: Just smaller generally. Small orchestra, played in a small theatre. It's a very intimate show about emotions and subtle things, and if it gets too big, you lose the subtleties, and if you lose the subtleties you lose the entire show.

MA: Your most recent musical was *Working*. What made you decide to use Studs Terkel's book as a basis for a musical? Why did you decide to bring in other composers[18] to do the score instead of doing it all yourself?

SS: I don't think anyone can really answer what makes him decide to do something. I loved that book.

---

[17] Topol played the leading role of Aimable until replaced late in the tryout by Paul Sorvino. Carole Demas played Genevieve until eventually replaced by Patti Lupone

[18] In addition to Schwartz, James Taylor, Craig Carnelia, Micki Grant, Mary Rodgers and Susan Birkenhead all contributed to the score.

I was very, very affected by it. I liked the whole idea. I knew I wanted to do that before I'd even read the book. I saw an announcement of the book in a little leaflet from the Book-of-the-Month club and I immediately knew that I wanted to do that. I can't even explain that. I felt when I sat down to really try and adapt it that for me to try and write all the scores, all the music, there would be many, many times when I would essentially be doing pastiche because I'd be imitating other styles that might be right for the character, and after a while it began to occur to me that maybe I'd better invite some people who wrote more naturally in those styles to participate.

MA: Like James Taylor?

SS: I went right to the people that I liked.

MA: How did the show do critically?

SS: Well, sort of mixed. I feel there were some problems with the Broadway production, but I think it's the best show I've ever done. I really like it, and a lot of the critics didn't. Some of them liked it very much, but not enough of them, and not enough of the critics who wrote for the more influential papers liked it to keep it running. Again, that is another show that has been done many, many times since the Broadway production, always very successfully.

MA: Where?

SS: All over the place. Do you want me to start listing cities for you? I think there have been so far about 20-25 productions.

MA: One question which the Artistic Director of the Arts Club asked is whether you would consider starting a show with a regional theatre, like the Arts Club?

SS: Oh, I would only consider starting a show – were I ever to do another show I would only consider starting a show with a regional theatre. I would never do a show directly for New York.

MA: What's next?

SS: I don't really know. I sort of take things one step at a time. Right now I'm involved in trying to get the *Magic Show* transferred to film, and have that work as a film. I know that will take – by the time we're done with the filming and the editing and the post-scoring etc. that's bound to take pretty much through the rest of the year, or at least until holidays when I don't like to work anyway. And then, I don't know, so I just will wait and see what happens.

MA: It seems that through *Godspell*, *Magic Show* and *Working*, you've developed a recognisable style for small, very personal musicals as opposed to large budget shows that merely attempt to overwhelm. Do you see that as continuing to be viable?

SS: I write what I'm interested in, in the style that appeals to me. I tend to be interested in this sort of thing, so I suspect that that's the way I will continue to go. I don't mean to say I wouldn't do a big, large-scale show if I felt that that's what I wanted to do, but I don't set out to deliberately have a style or to do something a certain way. I just set out to do a specific job. I mean there would be a specific idea I'm interested in, and I try to realise that as well as I know how.

MA: Sort of whatever suits your mood?

SS: Yeah, and I feel it dictates its own style.

MA: I understand you've become an author of children's books.

SS: Well, I haven't become an author of children's books. I did write a children's book called *The Perfect Peach*[19] which is published by Little Brown, because the illustrator – a guy named Leonard Lubin, an artist that I admired very much. He asked me if I'd like to collaborate with him on something and I said I would so I did, but that's not really a career that I'm expecting to pursue. The pictures are absolutely marvelous. I will say that, since I had nothing to do with them!

---

[19] Stephen Schwartz, *The Perfect Peach*, Little Brown & Co., New York, 1977.

At this point, the formal interview was concluded. I had sent him a promo record for *Broadway Melodies*, which highlighted the musicals of Leonard Bernstein, his collaborator on *Mass*. "Incidentally", he said, "I did bring the record that you sent me over to Lenny." I apologised for a couple of errors and oversights, including the fact that the program made no reference to *1600 Pennsylvania Avenue*. "Well, I think he'd just as soon you hadn't referred to that. I don't think he'll be disappointed that you didn't refer to it."

Only years later would I realise how close Stephen Schwartz had come to giving up show business. From the unfortunate demise of *Working* in 1978 until he began to work on *Rags* in 1982, he did very little, apart from the *Magic Show* movie and a TV adaptation of *Working*. In fact, according to Carole de Giere's biography, he rarely left his house. She writes, "In those pre-Internet days, he had no way of being bolstered by an audience who cared for his work. A trickle of letters came in from fans who wrote him in care of the theatre, which he appreciated."[20] After my interview, I began a correspondence with him that lasted for the next couple of decades. Long before he began teaching workshops for ASCAP, I was sending him my demo tapes and scripts. In one letter from 1981, he wrote "Let me start right off by saying I think you have a very good start on something here. I particularly think that as a composer, you show enormous promise – you have a wonderful gift for

---

[20] Carole de Giere, *Defying Gravity – the Creative Career of Stephen Schwartz from Godspell to Wicked*, Applause Theatre and Cinema Books, New York, 2008, p.175.

melody, great musicality, a good sense of how to use a chorus to make a song interesting; in short, I feel you have the potential for a real career as a theatre composer. Lucky you - such talents are rarer than you know." I cannot overstate what that comment meant to me. Of course, he was sometimes blunt in his criticisms. He was honest about what he thought, which only made the positive comments more meaningful.

I actually met Stephen in person for the first time a few weeks after that initial interview when I visited the set of the *Magic Show* movie, which was directed by a future mentor of mine, Norman Campbell, a composer in his own right. (He had scored the long-running Canadian musical *Anne of Green Gables*.) The next time I met him in person was some twenty years later when I saw him at a fringe production of *Pippin* at the Bridewell Theatre in London. This production included a revised ending in which Theo, Pippin's adopted son, sings a reprise of "Corner of the Sky", suggesting that he too had the wanderlust gene. Schwartz was so impressed by this that it was incorporated into the 2013 Broadway revival. The last time I saw him was in 2003 when I attended a preview of *Wicked* while in New York working on my own musical, *A Little Princess*. We still occasionally exchange emails, although he is a little busier now than he was back in 1980.

To Dance, Perhaps to Dream

When *A Chorus Line* premiered Off-Broadway   at the Neuman Theatre in Greenwich Village, it was the talk of the town even before its opening night. Somebody had finally produced a musical for and about Broadway dancers. Since that time, *A Chorus Line* has become one of the legends of the musical theatre, and every dancer dreams of the opportunity to join its ranks.

When I recently received a notice from the Fifth Avenue Theatre in Seattle saying that they would be holding open auditions for all companies of *A Chorus Line,* I immediately seized the opportunity to gather together a group of Vancouver's most talented young dancers. I began by notifying all the dance studios and talent agencies, and then phoned a number of dancers whom I knew personally.

I was told that a number of Canadians had tried to audition for this show before, but were turned away for lack of a US work permit. Several phone calls and a fair amount of persuasion solved this problem — I was assured by *Chorus Lines* press representative Bill Wilson that there would be no problems with Canadians auditioning.

A Chorus Line has already had a number of Canadians in its various companies over the past six years. The first of these was Vancouver-born Jeff Hyslop, who played the role of Mike in both the London and Broadway companies. "I auditioned like every other person for that show," recalls Hyslop. "At the time, they'd auditioned 3500 people. Michael Bennett and (co-choreographer) Bob Avian had 400 people in Toronto audition. I was choreographing *Company* for David Y.H. Lui here for his new theatre, and I flew out on the Sunday, which was our day off, and David gave me the Monday as well. So I auditioned on the Monday, and after the audition Bernie Gersten, the associate producer, congratulated me and said, 'I'll see you in New York.'"

Very early in the Seattle auditions, it became apparent that the casting people were looking for certain ' types', such as a short Chinese girl, a Puerto Rican boy, etc. The audition began by dividing the dancers into calls of ten each, and lining them up on stage. This was just so that Production Stage Manager Bud Coffey and Dance Captain Alex MacKay (also a

Vancouver native) could eye the people and choose the ones who might have the right 'look' .The girls were auditioned first. Each girl said her name, age, and where she was from, then had to demonstrate a double pirouette and a time step.

From the first call, five of the ten were from our group. Teryl Rothery, Pamela Quick, Denise Kask, Inga Pederson and Barbera Tutt went onto the stage, trying their best not to appear nervous. Standing in a line on the show's set, with the back wall of the stage covered in huge mirrors it's like a scene from the show has come full circle.

Inga and Teryl were asked to stay for a second audition, while the rest were thanked and encouraged to keep studying, keep dancing. Failure to be called back is no reflection on the dancer's talent. They may be tremendous performers, but were not the 'type' wanted for this show. The second call included Darcelle Chan and Charlene Chan (no relation). Both of these girls were asked to stay.

The second stage of the audition was a ballet combination, which is related to the opening dance of the show. For this, the dancers were divided into groups of three and put through a rigorous routine designed to make or break them. None of the Vancouver girls were called back this time. For Teryl, things might have been different if they'd asked for a jazz combination.

These dancers are no newcomers to their trade.

Several have been featured in local commercials and musicals. Teryl appeared as a dancer on the Tom *Jones TV* series, while Pamela has been seen in several Vancouver productions. Inga has been studying in New York at the American Musical and Dramatic Academy and danced in Macy's Parade.

The men's audition was basically the same as the women's. Keith Quong, Greg Templeton, Hernando Cortez, Ken Blaschuk and Jerry Pender went into the first group, from which Jerry, Hernando and Greg were asked to come back.

At this point, like the characters in the show, I asked them why they like to dance.

"I'm an exhibitionist!" shouted Jerry. "I love dancing. It feels good." Jerry, at 26, is among the most experienced of the group, having appeared in numerous commercials and TV shows, in addition to the musicals *Pippin, The Boyfriend,* and *Pyjama Game.*

Ken, up until two years ago, was a competitive runner, but after cracking a disc in his spine, had to find an alternative form of physical activity. "I was dancing to get some flexibility back, and I just sort of kept going." Teryl has always liked to dance. "I always used to do it at home, so I thought I'd take some classes." However, for Vancouver's dancers, getting an opportunity to perform is not that easy. When I asked people their ambitions, a few said "to be a star," but many just wanted to be able to make a living doing what they love most.

It was now time for Greg, Jerry and Hernando to go back on stage for their ballet combinations. After a tense twenty minutes, the production stage manager and the dance captain put their heads together to choose who would be called back again. Three men were asked to stay for a singing audition, one being Hernando.

After finishing the song he had prepared, Hernando was asked to sing one of the songs from the show, "I Hope I Get It". Hernando and the other two were then told that they might be called back for an audition with the New York casting director. If he was not called he would not be in the show.

Hernando has not so far been called back, but he was very pleased to have made it thus far. At seventeen, he was the second youngest of our group, and the only one to make it to the final stage. He credits Vancouver choreographer Grace Macdonald with starting his career. "She made me love it all. She taught me everything."

Soon after the Audition, Hernando left for New York on a scholarship to study theatre at the State University of New York. Inga will also be returning to New York to study. Keith will be appearing in *Chicago* at the Metro Theatre, while Ken and Greg recently appeared in *From Broadway with Love* at the Playhouse. The rest of them will return to their regular routine of auditions, classes, some commercials, and the odd stage musical, building up impressive resumes. Why do they do it?

As Jerry said, "I feel the best when I'm on stage."

The original version of this article appeared in the October 1982 issue of *Playboard Magazine*, Vancouver.

Postscript: After working as a dancer for Folies Bergère and the Radio City Music Hall Rockettes, Inga Pederson McLaughlin returned to Vancouver. Greg Templeton studied at American Musical & Dramatic Academy, but also returned to Vancouver. Hernando earned his Bachelor's of Fine Arts at Purchase College Conservatory of Dance and later joined Mikhail Baryshnikov's White Oaks Dance Project before forming his own company in New York. Teryl Rothery became well known as a recurring actress on the television series *Stargate SG-1*. Sadly, Jerry Pender was lost to AIDS.

The Banff Centre:
Music Theatre's Leading Edge

Webster's New Twentieth Century Dictionary defines a musical as "a theatrical production consisting of musical numbers, dances and humorous or satirical skits, centred upon some slight plot and usually having elaborate costuming and staging." The same dictionary defines opera as "a play having all or most of its text set to music, with arias, recitatives, choruses, duets, trios, etc. sung to orchestral accompaniment, usually characterized by elaborate costuming, scenery and choreography." Both of these labels are very limiting. Stephen MacNeff, associate artistic director of the Banff Centre's Music Theatre Studio Ensemble, sees both of these as a part of the broader field of Music Theatre. "It's a fairly broad term," MacNeff explains. 'The simplest definition, really, is any kind of lyric stage activity that has music and where the dramatic component is as important as the musical component."

Although the term Music Theatre has been in music dictionaries for some time, it has only recently come into common usage. It is most frequently used to describe avant-garde works, such as COMUS Music Theatre's recent world premiere of R. Murray Schaeffer's *RA* in Toronto.

The Ensemble began under the direction of Artistic Director Michael Bawtree in. September

1981, after a successful six week experiment one year earlier. The first group has now reached the end of their two-year programme, and Bawtree recently held auditions for a new ensemble, most of whom will have had previous professional experience. Some of his students are opera singers, some are pop singers, some are actors and some dancers. They're all brought together to learn the balance of their craft, so that actors may learn to sing and singers learn to act. Stephen MacNeff explains, 'The bottom line of our programme is training, and at the same time training people to take a kind of refreshed attitude toward the work that they do, so that when they go back out into the business, they can get work in some of the more exciting things that are going on."

The programme also includes a number of writers, composers, designers and directors who work together to commission new works for the ensemble. In its first 18 months, the ensemble has produced seventeen works, ranging from small-scale, one act pieces to the recent premiere of *Sasha*, a musical romance by Stephen Oliver, the English composer who was responsible for the words and music of *Nicholas Nickleby* on Broadway. In addition, they have performed such twentieth century classics as Kurt Weill and Bertold Brecht's *The Rise and Fall Of The City Of Mahagonny*.

Sasha is by far the most ambitious of the new works that the programme has presented, and the Banff Centre will retain an interest long after it has left their stage. They are actively soliciting productions of the piece, both on stage and television, and have exclusive North American rights to the show. The creators will approach both opera companies and popular musical theatre producers. They feel they can make the crossover between opera and musical theatre with ease, because they see themselves in a cosmopolitan context. 'The world is such a small place, these days," says MacNeff. "As soon as Andrew LIoyd Webber puts on *Cats,* we know about it the next day or the next week. It's not like we have to wait for a number of years to see these things. So because we have a much greater degree of accessibility to them, I tend to think of it as being a fairly global movement. There are a number of people all over the world who are working in such a way, and taking a particular kind of attitude of philosophy, which says this is a new way of looking at music. For instance, it is no accident that someone like Stephen Oliver came to write *Sasha* for us, because he had worked with Trevor Nunn on *Nicholas Nickleby* for the Royal Shakespeare Company. Trevor Nunn was the director of *Cats.* Stephen Oliver wrote *Sasha* for us, he was directed by Colin Graham, so it's a kind of international network of people. I think one of the nice things about doing *Sasha* in Banff is that it helps to include both ourselves, the Banff Centre, our participants and Canada as a whole in part of an international network of activity."

Banff's Music Theatre programme is the only one of its kind in the Western world. Students come from all over North America and Europe to auditions held in London, New York, Los Angeles, San Francisco, Toronto, Montreal, Edmonton, Calgary and Vancouver. Their annual tuition is approximately $8500, although the actual cost of the programme is closer to $25,000 per student. The balance is made up out of corporate donations and grants from the Province of Alberta.

Theirs is an approach that may be quite radical in terms of opera, but the concept of music and drama having the same weight is not new to the musical theatre. Ever since *Oklahoma* opened in 1943, this has been accepted as a basic principle on Broadway. Since then, musicals and opera have been gradually drifting together, with musicals like *Evita* and *Sweeney Todd* taking on the characteristics of opera, while works such as Leonard Bernstein's *Mass* and Carlisle Floyd's *Willie Stark* have begun to look more like Broadway.

What the Music Theatre programme seeks to do is commendable. They seek to find a new, perhaps distinctly Canadian, approach to Music Theatre and to explore the possibilities of the field. This comes through a long process of experimentation and a study of what has been accomplished previously. However, it is a slow process of evolution. "I think evolve is the right term to use," says MacNeff, "because 'evolve' suggests that there is time involved. I think the element of time is one of the most important. One can't expect things to be major world successes, whatever they might be, overnight.

The programme at Banff is now only going into its third year. When we started up here, we had a lot of things to figure out and a lot of problems to solve. I can't say what we'll be doing five or ten years from now, and even then, I wouldn't give any guarantees."

This article originally appeared in *Playboard Magazine*, Vancouver, in 1983.

The Music Theatre Studio Ensemble operated from 1981 until 1989.

Reid Shelton: Minding the Store

Reid Shelton (1924-1997) was best known for originating the part of Daddy Warbucks in *Annie*, but his career ranged from *My Fair Lady* (in which he played or understudied the role of Freddie Eynsford-Hill) to the Leonard Bernstein/Alan Jay Lerner flop *1600 Pennsylvania Avenue*, where he was befriended by producer Roger Stevens, who became a mentor. (It is said that he modeled his betrayal of Daddy Warbucks on Stevens, who was one of the show's producers.)[21]

I interviewed him on 11 June 1982 at the Fifth Avenue Theatre in Seattle, where he was playing Warbucks in the touring production of *Annie*. The interview was for Lyndon Grove's program *Man About Town* on CHQM-FM, Vancouver. Clearly the ticket prices and budget figures mentioned reflect that time.

Mel Atkey: Reid, the opening at the Goodspeed Opera House – I'm very interested in knowing some of the metamorphosis that *Annie* went through.

Reid Shelton: Well, metamorphosis – doesn't that word mean something that's dead that comes back to life? This is just a "borning", more of a creation than a metamorphosis. *Annie*, the first script, was I thought a very good script, but it had problems, as any script does when you go out of town. And I took

---

[21] Ralph Blumenthal, "Reid Shelton, Actor, 72, Dies; Original Broadway Warbucks", *New York Times*, 10 June 1997.

this job because they said it was being done as a pre-Broadway tryout situation. I've learned over the years that because you do something as a Broadway tryout doesn't mean you're necessarily going to do it on Broadway. So when we got up there, we started rehearsing it and very early on there were things in the script that were apparent that needed to be changed. In the first script, I come in, I meet the child, and I say "But you're not a boy" and she said "No, I'm not" and I said "but you're an adorable little girl!" Well, the play is over! That's what the play is about, so you see it was over before it got started. And so, early on we discovered that. There were several other things throughout the script [that] are gone or so forth that were tried out there. Now I think that one of the main reasons for the success of this show is that every scene and every joke and every moment was tried in front of an audience, and the audiences are the only ones that can tell you what works and what doesn't work. Thomas Meehan, the author was able to craft a script in the very best circumstances by being able to play it for – I think we were up there all in all eleven weeks with rehearsal time – seven weeks playing, three weeks rehearsal [sic] to make a script with the audience telling him what's working.

MA: Was there any difference in the story line at that point?

RS: Yes. When Annie ran away, she ran into a beanery or a diner… and she gets a job as a dishwasher. The man who runs the place is not a very nice man and he turns her in to get a reward.

That scene was cut, and the Hooverville scene was put in.

MA: Was there a number in the beanery scene?

RS: Yes, it was "We've Got Annie", which is now in the movie, which I guess is Ann Reinking's number.

MA: I know when you first played Daddy Warbucks you did it with hair, didn't you?

RS: Yes, yes.

MA: Did you find that it made a difference in your feeling for the character?

RS: Not at all. Not in the least. It merely was that someone along the line said, "But he's not bald." If I'd have said "No, I won't cut my hair", everybody would be playing it with hair now. But I don't have any great feelings about that. I feel you have to do for each job what's necessary for that job. They felt that it was kind of necessary for me to shave my head so I did it.

MA: Do you think you'll keep it that way after *Annie*?

RS: I have no idea. It depends on how the people who hire actors perceive me.

MA: The stage, I understand, at the Goodspeed has some pretty severe technical limitations.

RS: It's tiny. I don't know in feet, but it's a tiny, tiny stage. And there's no wing space. It was like a little presentation house in the 1800s. I think it was built, if I'm not mistaken, either just before the Civil War or just after the Civil War.[22] It was Goodspeed's Landing. Mr. [William] Goodspeed built it. It was a commercial venture. It was a theatre with shops and a bar and I think they even had some hotel rooms in another building, but it was all Goodspeed's Landing. Now, East Haddam [Connecticut] now is merely a few gift shops, a gas station, a grocery store and this lovely old building which – I think it may be a national monument now, I'm not sure.[23]

MA: Where do they get their audiences from?

RS: It's quite a resort area, and a lot of very well-to-do people have summer homes up there. It's very near Easton, Connecticut. It's right on the Connecticut River. They even draw people from Hartford, which is not too far away.

MA: Do the New York critics normally come out to Goodspeed?

RS: Yes, they do. Of course I think Goodspeed encourages it and pays the bills, you know what I mean? There is a kind of interesting story – the two men that run the Shubert Organization[24] four or five times had a plane waiting for them to come up and

---

[22] 1877.

[23] Listed on the U.S. National Register of Historic Places, 1971.

[24] Bernard B. Jacobs, Gerald Schoenfeld

see the show hoping perhaps that they would put us on Broadway, and they never showed up, so out about I imagine fifty million dollars because of that, not taking the time to go see the show!

MA: But Mike Nichols did see it.

RS: Now, you asked about people who live up there – Mike has a place up there. And right next door to Mike is Jay Presson Allen and Lewis Allen. Jay Presson Allen – do you know the name?[25] She is now producing and writing movies. Marvellous woman. And she saw the show, and she was the one who called Mike Nichols and said, "You have to see this show," and got him to come see it. And Mike saw our director and lyricist Martin Charnin afterwards and Martin said, "What do you think of it, Mike?" and he said "What do I think of it? I want to produce it on Broadway!" And that was how we got into the aegis of Mike Nichols.

MA: How long did it take from that point to actually getting the production going?

RS: To get it to Broadway?

MA: Yeah, raising the capital, etc.

RS: Well, he said that in, say, early October and we went into rehearsal in January.

---

[25] She wrote – among many other things – the screenplay for the film version of *Cabaret*.

MA: These things actually sometimes start out going into rehearsals without knowing if they're actually going to be able to open, don't they?

RS: Of course, any show you don't know whether someone's going to pick you up. Nell Nugent, who's now producing all these things on Broadway who produced *Nicholas Nickleby* and so forth – she came up for Mr. [James] Nederlander and she put a negative report in. And so when Nederlander finally did put money in the show through Roger Stevens, Nell didn't have a job any more. I don't know whether she was fired or she decided to leave, but of course it was the making on Nell Nugent because she started producing on her own. There's another kind of wonderful story – Nederlander was kind of coerced in a way into putting $125,000 into *Annie* because Roger Stevens said "I'm going in for $250,000 and you're going to come in and we'll play the Alvin Theatre." So Jimmy evidently, so the story goes, was wringing his hands – "What have I done?" – and he went to a woman named Gladys Rackmil[26] and said "Gladys, why don't you take $25,000 of it?" She said, "Oh no, I don't want to." So after we were a hit, she literally did – and she tells this story herself – write a cheque for $25,000 and takes it up to Jimmy and throws it on his desk and says, "I'll take $25,000 of it!"

MA: That reminds me apparently Martin Charnin got a telegram from Stuart Ostrow saying that he cried twice in the performance – once when he heard

---

[26] Gladys Rackmil was James Nederlander's sister-in-law.

"Maybe" and the second time was when he realised he wasn't producing it.

RS: That sounds like something Stuart would say. But they all had a chance to take it. Everybody was approached and nobody wanted it. So, it was Roger Stevens who was the head of the Kennedy Center – and he was very active here in Seattle – Roger had the faith in it, or whatever, and he put $250,000, but he had financial control. He's really the man who says what we do and what we don't do, in the final analysis. And out of that $250,000, the Kennedy Center will have made over six and a half million from it so far.

MA: Was there, in the beginning with *Annie*, any real intuitive feeling among the cast that this show was a hit?

RS: I always felt it was, but I also felt that it depends on who brings us in. I mean we could have been brought in by a lesser producer than Mike Nichols and Lewis Allen – and Jimmy Nederlander and Roger Stevens, and we wouldn't have done as well.

MA: It does seem to me that *Annie* is the kind of a show in which it's a very good show but it's very easy to interpret the wrong way.

RS: Yeah!

MA: I know one of the things that Martin [Charnin] was very worried about is that it was going to be played camp.[27]

RS: Oh, yes. No, and I also would never – I play it absolutely for real, always. If you perceive it as camp, that's your problem, or it's your perception. But if we had played it for camp, we would have killed it completely. It must be real. Any camp show must be real. For instance, the minute *The Boy Friend* is played for camp you don't have a show. You have – I don't know what. A mess. But if you really believe that this girl – and I can remember Julie [Andrews] when she would take that pose that it was so real. You felt for her. And that feeling is what's so important. I don't believe you can ever play camp, ever, because camp is perceived by every person differently, so you can't satisfy all that. You've got to have a core to play any play, and that core is reality. You as the audience can get whatever you want out of a show. You can take home whatever you want, but the actors, producers, directors must constantly have the core that they want to tell of the story they want to tell.

MA: In other words, whether it's real to the audience or not, it has to be real to the character.

RS: That's right, exactly.

---

[27] *Annie* composer Charles Strouse's earlier comic-book based musical *It's A Bird... It's A Plane... It's Superman*, directed by Harold Prince, was played for camp. It closed after 129 performances.

MA: What were some of your previous Broadway experiences before *Annie*?

RS: well, right before *Annie* I did a thing called *1600 Pennsylvania Avenue* which was Alan Jay Lerner and Leonard Bernstein, and it was a terrible fiasco. I don't think it needed to be, but it was. And the oversimplification of why it failed I think was true: it was an idea that didn't work. What they wanted to do was tell the first hundred years of the White House in a musical comedy, and to do it in a rehearsal situation. So we'd come on in rehearsal clothes and by the end of the show we're in complete costume. Now that sounds like a wonderful concept, but when you're dealing with a hundred years, it's very difficult to do that. The first number was George Washington and ended up with Theodore Roosevelt. Now, I thought there were some marvelous things in the show. But, we went into rehearsal without a completed script, and the director[28] was signed two weeks before we started to rehearse, so that he was not part of the gesticulation of making a show. From the very beginning I felt that we had a problem, to say the least.

MA: When you say you thought it was one that didn't need to fail, do you think, like you were talking about with *Annie*, that it was something that depended on who mounted it?

RS: Well, there were mistakes made in the production. I mean, [Roger] Stevens and [Robert]

---

[28] Frank Corsaro

Whitehead were the producers. But Tony Walton for instance did the costumes and scenery and he's a very good designer but I personally when I saw them thought they were ugly. Well, like the Emperor's new clothes, nobody would say to Tony that they're ugly. I mean, Tony was given a show to do and they should have said that. What Tony meant was there's a federal red – it's a kind of a wine maroon colour which was popular during Lincoln's time and that was the colour that was through the show and it was a dull colour – it just didn't work.

MA: What was your role?

RS: At one point I played several roles, I ended up with three or four. I played Admiral Cockburn, senator [Roscoe] Conkling – I can't remember the other – there's a couple more Senators – anyway they were good roles. I was the utility villain! The reason I think they hired me is I did the same thing in a show called *The Rothschilds* with Hal Linden and I played all the villains.

MA: Were you in the original cast of that?

RS: No, Keene Curtis[29] [was], and I replaced Keene after six months, and as it turned out, I played it for a whole year. Keene went off to make a movie, poor guy, and it was never released. And then he came into New York and replaced me [in *Annie*] while I went on vacation and then they hired him for this company that I'm with now and when that company

---

[29] 1923-2002

left Los Angles they asked me to come out and take over.

MA: I understand that you started out in a minor role in *My Fair Lady*.

RS: Minor? I was in the chorus! If you can be more minor than that! But I understudied Freddie [Eynsford-Hill] in the beginning, and it looked for about three days like the part was going to be mine but it never worked out. Then when they formed the national company I wrote Moss [Hart] and said I'd like to do it and he said "Nothing would please me more" – I still have that letter – and I toured with *My Fair Lady* for five years and two months and we played Seattle here and Vancouver – the Queen Elizabeth Theatre – I think we played there twice, or maybe even three times. I sang "On the Street Where You Live" 2100 times in that show.

MA: When would that be?

RS: '57 we opened the national company and I played until '64.

MA: You went to the USSR with that, didn't you?

RS: Yes, we did!

MA: I find it interesting to think of how *My Fair Lady* would go over in Russia.

RS: Well, I got a letter from an English teacher in Leningrad that kind of amused me. She said, "You play Freddie Eynsford-Hill as though he would take his rightful place in society," meaning that he would work and so forth. I didn't know I was doing that. I think Freddie is a bit of an ass but I played the fact that he was very much in love – you know, "puppy-love" kind of thing.

MA: Who was Higgins on the tour?

RS: We started out with Brian Aherne[30] and Anne Rodgers and then Michael Evans[31] took over and then a girl named Diane Todd – I can't remember. I worked with maybe four or five different Eliza's and three or four different Higgins's.

MA: You did *Carousel* at Lincoln Center.

RS: I did it at Lincoln's Center and I did it at Jones Beach[32] [in Wantagh, New York]. I've done, all-in-all, nine productions of *Carousel* playing Mr. Snow.

MA: How did you start out on a career in musical theatre? Did you set out or did it just happen?

RS: Well, I had to make a living! Simple. I think the most successful actors are those that approach it as a living and a profession. I know so many young people today that want to be "stars". That's silly. Be

---

[30] 1902-86
[31] 1920-2007
[32] Jones Beach Marine Theatre, 1973

a good actor and you might be a star if you're lucky. I never went out to do any of that. I went out to make a living, and my career has constantly gone up. I've had bad times and good times – very few real bad times. I've made a living only from the theatre since 1951except for one period when I took another job not for the money but for my head. I was getting a divorce and I needed to reconcile all that with my life and I got a job as a computer programmer kind of thing, and I was only in that job six weeks. I got another job in the theatre and I went back and my head was cured and everything's fine ever since. But that was way back in the early '60s.

MA: How did you start?

RS: I have a Master's degree from the University of Michigan to teach voice and I taught there one year on a teaching fellowship. I loved the teaching, I didn't like the politics involved in a big university. I was twenty-eight years old, and I thought "If I don't try now I'll never know if I could do something in New York". I went to New York on a Monday and I got a job at Radio City Music Hall on Tuesday. I was there for about seven months and I went right from that into *Wish You Were Here*. This was in the chorus, the ensemble, but I would always end up with a speaking part. From that I went into *By the Beautiful Sea* with Shirley Booth, and from that I went into *The Saint of Bleecker Street*, the Gian Carlo Menotti opera which played Broadway, and then *Fair Lady*. And *Fair Lady* was six years.

MA; What was your first principal role?

RS: *Fair Lady*, Freddie. Now all this time I was playing stock. I was doing my first *Carousel*, *Brigadoon*, *South Pacific* came later, but those were the shows I was doing

MA: Getting back onto the opening at Goodspeed. I understand that the opening of *Annie* didn't appear on the surface to be the most promising thing in the world. What happened with that? I know that the reviews were mixed .

RS: Now, everybody says that. C'mon. I did not perceive them as that way. For what we were at that time they were very good notices. We were a "work in progress" as they say nowadays, and I thought we were in very good shape. Our opening night was a disaster merely because there was a hurricane – I mean a real honest-to-God hurricane ripped through there. The power was out and all that kind of thing. But all of that, I think, helped in a way. It made people work. And I must say about Marty Charnin, I've never known a man work so hard as Marty has on this property. If this property makes him a millionaire he deserves every penny. His heart and soul went into this show. He almost was driven. It was just incredible to see someone so willing something to be good. He's a workaholic to begin with. The fact that we started out with this big storm was always taken as an omen. Well I don't believe in that kind of thing. However East Haddam is very into witches and all that sort of thing. You know Tom

Tryon wrote *The Other* [and *Harvest Home*] about that
area which had to do with that feeling –like there was
a man in east Haddam who had a safety pin through
his ear supposed to be to keep away evil spirits. He
was a man in his seventies. And the topography of
the area and the hills and so forth made it a place
where a lot of witches would hang out. So maybe
that's why we're a success. I don't know.

MA: Whenever you're looking at a show and
everyone is nervous about how the opening is going
to go you can say, well here's *Annie,* one of the most
successful shows on Broadway and it still had its
problems on opening night.

RS: Oh, well that's just the one problem. I mean the
raising the money was – Marty doesn't like to tell this
story, but we went to rehearsal Monday and Tuesday
and there was no money. We hadn't signed our
contracts. It wasn't until Roger Stevens put his name
on the dotted line that we could rehearse.

MA: Was this at Goodspeed or Kennedy Center?

RS: Kennedy Center. And it's so painful [for] Marty
that he never tells that story. In other words, a bond
has to be posted. Until someone signs their name that
the unions will accept, you can't rehearse. So we sat
Monday and Tuesday and couldn't rehearse. On
Wednesday we started to rehearse.

MA: This is why I asked when you started rehearsals if you knew it was going to open, because I think they only had a little over half the budget raised.

RS: Also I think that was good. It all came on to Marty's shoulders, but we came in for $800,000. Now, you know what they're costing on Broadway now – three million, which is stupid. That's just a waste. That's because it's not managed, you know what I mean?

MA: What would make them cost that?

RS: Oh, extra lights, costumes that really don't contribute that much, wigs that don't contribute that much, orchestrations that don't contribute that much. They think if they spend three million dollars they're going to have a good show, and that's not true. This show is good because we didn't spend three million dollars.

MA: They spent forty million on the movie.

RS: I won't comment on that! I think Tommy Meehan said it best. He said "I wrote a story about Christmas and this isn't a story about Christmas." And all those circus performers? Come on! I want to get back to this budget thing, because I think it's very interesting. They say to the public "We spent three million dollars, you've got to pay $40 to see it." I can remember Marty sitting behind the production table saying, "Well we can cut that... we can cut that... He cut $2300 out of the wig plot. Now, you know, the wig plot is how many wigs you need on the show. I wear the same suit at the opening of the second act, and I always have because at Goodspeed I did it, but it saved them the price of my suit, which are about $600-$700. But my favourite part of that is – we opened in Washington DC and the scenery was not painted. Now, had we flopped, they would have saved $150,000. What Roger Stevens had to see is if the show was really going to make it. He came back at intermission, our opening night in Washington, and said "Paint the scenery". Now that's a show business story, but it's absolutely true. He deliberately was not going to spend that money until he saw what he had. Then Mike [Nichols] put the silk on the mansion walls, which were just white walls. The Hannigan was all white because they hadn't painted it. We didn't have the pictures [on the walls] because they came about $400 apiece. A girl came backstage and painted all those masterpieces. And I admire that! I admire that, because that is watching the store. That's what theatre should be about, so that you can give the public the maximum amount. Now we resisted, in New York, raising the ticket price. Our show was the one that resisted all that. And then finally they had to go along with it.

MA: It would be pretty hard for a show like *Annie*, with those ticket prices, to survive when it's a family show.

RS: I know exactly what you're saying, but families go and see these other shows at that price if they want to go. There are several shows in New York right now that, if the ticket price was cheaper, yes I'd go. And there are others that I'd say I'd go no matter what it costs.

MA: Aside from your role in *Annie*, what would you consider to be your greatest experience on stage?

RS: I'm asked that all the time. I always love the part I'm playing at the moment, or I wouldn't be playing it. Career-wise, of course, Daddy Warbucks is the most wonderful thing I've ever done. I love *Carousel*. But I did a play by David Storey called *The Contractor* and I loved that. I also did a little off-Broadway play called *Man with a Load of Mischief*, which the audience seemed to like. More people stop me on the street and congratulate me who remember that show than even this show.

MA: Do you find any kind of a problem being recognised on the street?

RS: Not really. Most people are very nice. The only thing I sometimes get a little uptight about is after a matinee when I'm tired and people want autographs then and there's a whole slew of kids and they're pulling at you and so forth, I find that kind of frightening. Not frightening – but I mean annoying, I should say. But most of the time everyone is more than considerate.

Reid Shelton passed away as the result of a stroke in Portland, Oregon in 1997.

"MEL, YOU'RE PANICKING!"
— In New York with Bob Sickinger

Not long after I arrived in London from Toronto in 1991, I found myself in the returns queue for a Discover the Lost Musicals presentation of Frank Loesser's 1960 flop *Greenwillow* at the Theatre Museum. An elderly bearded American and I were vying for the last ticket. As it turned out, we both got in. When he learned that I was a composer and lyricist, he offered to buy me dinner.

He told me that he used to run a youth theatre in Chicago in the early '60s, and that playwright David Mamet – along with *Grease* creators Jim Jacobs & Warren Casey – had been among his protégés. I could barely conceal my scepticism, until he showed me the *Vanity Fair* article in which Mamet proclaimed, "Bob Sickinger was one of the greatest directors I've ever known", adding "He invented the Chicago theatre of today."[33]

And there were others who agreed with him. "Mr. Sickinger was something of a Pied Piper", Bruce Weber later wrote in the *New York Times*, "an alluring, commanding personality with an irresistible idea: that theatre isn't presented to a community but arises from it."[34] "To the extent that any individual founded off-Loop theatre", says *Chicago Tribune* critic Chris Jones, "a case can be made that Sickinger was that man."[35] It was from these roots that companies like Steppenwolf grew.

Fast-forward to twelve years later (2003), and there is another returns queue. This time, I'm in New York, and the production is *A Little Princess*. The run had almost entirely sold out in the 99 seat Wings Theatre. This time, I was the composer-lyricist, and Bob the book writer and director.

In many respects, we were opposites – I like subtlety, whereas Bob was bombastic. (One of his nicknames

[33] David Mamet, "Why I Write for Chicago Theatre", *Vanity Fair*, November 1984.

[34] Bruce Weber, "Bob Sickinger, Chicago Stage Innovator, Dies at 86", *New York Times*, 14 May 2013.

[35] Chris Jones, "Robert Sickinger, Pioneer of Chicago Theater Dies at 86", *Chicago Tribune*, 9 May 2013.

was "The truck driver of the American Theatre".) After Bob visited me at the London theatre where I worked at the time, my manager approached me, exasperated, and said, "Are **all** Americans like him?!" In the interest of taste, brevity and conservation of rain forests, I have edited out his profanities. (This is the man who claimed to have taught David Mamet how to cuss.) In the 1960s, he brought the plays of Samuel Becket and Eugene Ionescu to Chicago's Hull House settlement, a centre for social reform and cultural enlightenment founded in 1886 by Jane Addams and Ellen Gates Starr. According to Mamet's *Vanity Fair* article, "Sickie exuded drama. He had a boundless passion for Beauty on the Stage and a complete conviction that said beauty was just and exactly what he **said** it was."

Now, instead of *Waiting for Godot*, we were doing a little girl's musical not a million miles away from *Annie*, but his rules were the same.

This was not our first attempt at writing together. Two years earlier, I had written seven songs for his adaptation of Willa Cather's novel *O Pioneers!* It was then that he proposed turning Frances Hodgson Burnett's classic story of a once-wealthy orphan into a musical. An admirer of the Marsha Norman/Lucy Simon musical *The Secret Garden* —also adapted from Burnett – I embraced the idea, even though Bob hated that *Secret Garden* – "too many *%@+ing ghosts".

Bob's plan was to reset the story from Victorian London to Civil War Washington, which I thought sounded like a workable plan. There had been a number of film and TV adaptations (and, we later learned, other musicals were in the works) but the only one I had seen was one from the early 1990s starring Eleanor Bron.

I prefer to begin by finding the emotional core of the show, and writing a song that embraces that, so as soon as Bob emailed the first scraps of dialogue, I wrote "Keep Up Your Chin", a farewell duet between Sara Crewe and her father, a colonel in the Union Army. First I emailed Bob the lyrics for approval, then I created the music (in a programme called Scorewriter) and faxed the score to Bob.

We met up face-to-face in London in late 2001, but once the Iraq War started, Bob, like many Americans, kept to his own side of the Atlantic, which meant that virtually all of our communication was by email, fax and the occasional tape. (Given the time of morning he liked to call, I had banned Bob from phoning me.)

It is important to note that the concept that went on stage was entirely Bob's. I was given an outline, indicating where songs should go and what they should say. In very few cases did I write a song where he had not indicated a place for one. Only one was discarded – for the opening scene, Colonel Crewe is drilling his troops, getting ready to go to war, and they are doting on his daughter Sara, the "little princess". Bob wanted martial music, but on the eve of the Iraq war, I was loath to write anything pro-military or jingoistic. I came up with "A Soldier with

Goodbye on His Mind", but it wasn't what Bob wanted. But Bob replied, "Audiences do love martial pageantry. Even pacifists such as ourselves, but we know better than to be seduced by it."[36] So I gave him a naïve flag-waver in which the soldiers sing proudly of "marching straight to heaven's door", then realise with horror what that implies: "That is to say 'we're happy', not 'we're dead'". So what if the irony goes over the audience's head, at least it's there.

It is when Sara is sent to Miss Minchin's School for Young Ladies that the story begins to move. Bob sent me a tape of a New Jersey cabaret singer named Patty Montano singing the best rendition of Stephen Schwartz's "The Hardest Part of Love" I've ever heard, and she was cast as Miss Minchin. (After hearing Minchin's first song, one of the people auditioning commented that, unlike Miss Hannigan in *Annie*, we had given Miss Minchin humanity.)

Because I would not be able to physically be there during rehearsals, it fell to the musical director, Mary Ann Ivan, to arrange the incidental music. Then, I arrived in New York in late October 2003, just as the show was beginning its first tech rehearsal. Bob was very anxious that I not usurp his authority, and decreed that all communication to the cast should come through him. But he had more pressing problems – the last group to use the theatre had not reinstalled the lighting board properly. In another corner, the mother of one of the children threatened to pull her daughter out of the show if the Wings staff

---

[36] Email to the author from Bob Sickinger dated 29 May 2002

didn't stop smoking backstage. The wardrobe mistress walked out into the street, let out a loud primal scream, then walked quietly back in, saying "I feel better now". That night, the cast didn't make it all the way through the show before stage manager Mark Glassberg stopped rehearsal (in accord with Equity rules) at eleven o'clock. I still didn't know how the ending worked.

The following night, the dress rehearsal, we finally came to the penultimate scene in which Sara finds her father in a veteran's hospital. The role of Sara was split between two actresses – Grace Clary and Kristin Danielle Klabunde (who had played Young Cosette in the final Broadway cast of *Les Misérables*). Bob had warned me previously that they had difficulty with the second act duet "A Mother to My Father", and I had sent a revised version which for some reason (like other changes) was never incorporated into the show. The song I heard I did not recognise. The chords had been radically changed, although the musical director maintained that was how she had received the music. (The danger of emailing MIDI files is that the music can be corrupted.) We called a last minute rehearsal for both girls to relearn the song in its original arrangement.

"Mel, you're panicking!" Bob shouted at me in the restaurant later. "This is not Broadway! We don't have a ten million dollar budget to fix things!" It doesn't cost ten million dollars to learn a song, I suggested. Then I sat through a long harangue about how I'm not living in the real world. I sat calmly as he exhorted me not to panic. Mamet wrote that "grown men and women lived in fear of [Bob's] wrath and blossomed at his praise." He also mentioned that he was "a maniac".

We made it through the preview largely intact. The next day, my entire family arrived from Vancouver. I brought them to the theatre early to set aside our seats. I asked a member of the staff if Bob was around. He rolled his eyes, saying "Use your ears! Does it **sound** like Bob is around?"

Our first review came out from Matthew Murray on a website called *Talking Broadway*. It was not good. After mentioning competing versions of the story by "talents as acclaimed as David Zippel and Andrew Lippa" he declared that our version "bears a somewhat less distinguished pedigree, and sets a standard the upcoming versions won't have much trouble surpassing." (As it turns out, neither the Zippel nor Lippa versions ever made it to Broadway.) "To best understand what this version is like, imagine an enterprising author rewriting *Annie* as an American folk musical in the British pop-opera mould, filling in the gaps with insights from Cliff's Notes of Burnett's book."[37] He seemed unhappy that we had not put the entire novel on stage.

But the audience felt differently – standing ovations every night, and virtually the entire run sold out in advance. Another review from *Show Business Weekly*

---

[37] Matthew Murray review of *A Little Princess*, Talkingbroadway.com, 24 October 2003

was more encouraging: "The songs, written by Mel Atkey, perfectly match the scenes. A banjo adds authentic American character while stately drum rolls introduce the Colonel. 'Keep Up Your Chin' carries an especially sweet melody and emphasises the importance of being optimistic." *Backstage*, New York's theatrical newspaper, wrote that "Mel Atkey's songs were catchy; I heard [the reviewer's daughter] Olivia humming them during intermission. Adapter-director Sickinger drew strong performances from his large and able cast."[38]

It was on the morning of my departure for London that we received the best news of all – quite unexpectedly, the *New York Times* had been to the show, and liked what they saw, saying that *A Little Princess* "has charm" and that I had composed "lovely music".[39]

Patty Montano had asked me to help her with her next cabaret show, and told me she wanted to include two of my *O Pioneers* songs on her next CD. Sadly, it was not to be. Shortly after the show finished, she was rushed into hospital, where she spent the next nine months. (She even got a get-well message from Stephen Schwartz, which impressed the nurses no end.) Early in 2004 she passed away at the age of only 44.

---

[38] Michael Lazan, *Backstage*, 25 November 2003

[39] Laurel Graeber, "Family Fare", *New York Times*, Friday 7 November 2003

"So what shall we do next?" asked Bob. "How about a musical version of *Waiting for Godot*?" I'm pretty sure he was kidding.

Although Bob asked me to work with him again – this time on a musical version of *Nicholas Nickleby* – it was not to be. Yes, we had our disagreements – as all collaborators do. However, even when we were arguing – or could it be **because** we were arguing? – I learned an awful lot from him. He believed in me and invested in me when nobody else would, and for that I will always be grateful. Bob Sickinger passed away in 2013 in Delray Beach, Florida.

A version of this article originally appeared under the title "Making it Happen" in *Musical Stages* in Spring, 2004.

Do Musicals Need Great Songs?

Legend has it that Broadway lyricist Ed Kleban disliked his song "What I Did for Love" so much that he left explicit instructions in his will that it not be sung at his memorial service. He would dismiss it with a curt "the money men made me do it".[40] While *A Chorus Line* composer Marvin Hamlisch was anxious for a "breakout" song that would have a life outside of the theatre, Kleban believed it was a sell-out. Why? "If a song interrupts the story telling in some way, it can damage the show", says John Sparks, artistic director of the Academy for New Musical Theatre in Los Angeles. "It's far more important that the music and lyrics give some insight into the character in the moment of the drama." It could be argued, however, that it is also important that certain key songs contain a strong melodic, rhythmic or lyrical "hook" in order to make an impression on the audience, thus "landing" their point. In his review of the National Theatre's production of *The Light Princess*, *Time Out*'s Andrzej Lukowski said it "doesn't really do the business in the tunes department where big things had been expected from songwriter Tori Amos... a couple of standalone showstoppers would have offered more oomph."[41]

So why is "What I Did for Love" in the show? Co-choreographer Bob Avian explains, "The first song

---

[40] Harry Haun, "What They Did For Love: *A Class Act* Comes to Broadway", Playbill.com, 1 March 2001

[41] *Time Out*, London, 15-21 October 2013.

that Marvin wrote that everybody loved, Michael [Bennett] more than anything, was 'At the Ballet'. And Michael turned to Ed Kleban and Marvin Hamlisch and said, 'That's the score.' What bothered Marvin ... was that it was so specific to *A Chorus Line* that it didn't have any commercial possibilities. It was all about the particular attitude in the context of the play. Every composer wants chart hits. And the whole score was becoming like that, whether it was 'Nothing' or 'The Montage' or 'At the Ballet' or 'God I Hope I Get It'. They were all plot-specific. And then when we got to the end of the play they wrote 'What I Did for Love'. [Hamlisch] pleaded with Michael to let [him] write this song that might have potential to be pulled outside the score... [Bennett] said, 'OK, see what you can come up with,' and they wrote that and Michael went, 'Oh OK,' and sure enough it happened to work because emotionally it was right even though it was a song of generalities. It works great."[42] John Sparks concedes, "I found it quite moving in the context of the show."

Of course, it could be argued that the most memorable song in that show is not "What I Did for Love" but "One", a diagetic showbiz promenade in the well-trodden tradition of Jerry Herman, Jule Styne and Cy Coleman.

Was Hamlisch's desire for a breakout song purely commercial, or does it fulfill a valid artistic purpose? The time was, from the 1920s through the 1950s,

---

[42] Jasper Rees, "10 Questions for Choreographer Bob Avian", TheArtsDesk.com, London, 20 Feb 2013.

when the classier hit songs all came from musicals – either Broadway or Hollywood. But those days are, for the most part, over. There have been the odd exceptions – Andrew Lloyd Webber managed to get Irish boy band Boyzone to record a cover version of "No Matter What" from *Whistle Down the Wind*, but it only proved the rule. Carly Simon released her version of "Not a Day Goes By" two months before *Merrily We Roll Along* opened in 1981, and Frank Sinatra similarly covered "Good Thing Going". Neither were major chart hits.

While hit parade songs may not come from stage musicals anymore, have we gone too far the other way? Seattle based librettist and playwright Stephen Oles sees a disturbing trend. "Theatre music and pop have gone off in their own direction, leaving pop song writing bereft of craft and intelligence… and theatre composers wandering off into increasingly sterile, etiolated idioms… Virtually every number is medium tempo. Melody is replaced by the repetition of short, uninteresting phrases of four or five notes – in the manner of Sondheim on an off day – and emotion, previously the essence of musical theatre, is eschewed as old-fashioned."

Even in the so-called Golden Age, writers and composers struggled with the demands of writing successful songs that worked both in and out of context. When composer and lyricist Hugh Martin wrote "Have Yourself a Merry Little Christmas" for the film *Meet Me in St. Louis* in 1944, his original lyrics went, "Have yourself a merry little Christmas / It may be your last/ Next year we may all be living in the past / Have yourself a merry little Christmas / Pop that champagne cork / Next year we may all be living in New York." [43] In the show's context, the family was distressed at the thought of leaving their home town. However, Judy Garland didn't want her character to sing such a dark lyric to her younger sister – she was supposed to be comforting her, not frightening her. Martin reluctantly changed it to the more familiar "Let your heart be light / Next year all our troubles will be out of sight". Even still, it contained the line "Until then we'll have to muddle through somehow." Only after Frank Sinatra persuaded Martin to change the line to "Hang a shining star upon the highest bough" for his 1957 recording did the song become the standard that we know today.

"The business of writing songs to become hits has never bothered me because I really don't know what makes a hit", said Stephen Sondhein in 1973. "And I have to tell you, it's a great relief not to worry about it any more. When Jule Styne and I wrote *Gypsy*, Jule was appalled when in 'Small World' I wrote a line that said, *"Funny, I'm a woman with children."* He said, 'Well, that means no man can sing the song.' I said, 'Jule, if I make the song general, then it's got no texture for the show at all. We've *got* a general song, 'You'll Never Get Away From Me,' that's general. 'Everything's Coming Up Roses', general. But here's this lady, she's trying to con this guy into handling

[43] Martin, Hugh (2010). *The Boy Next Door*. Trolley Press. pp. 196–197

her vaudeville act – and it's a con song. It's got to be terribly personalized.' Well, I changed the lyric for the printed music, the sheet music, so that a man could sing the song. But nowadays nobody has to worry about that sort of thing... I had a chance, I suppose, to make a hit song out of *Forum*, because 'Lovely' is a very pretty, easily hummable tune, and those were the days, back in 1962, when you were still occasionally listening to easily hummable tunes. But it's a comic show, and I can't have a straight song in a comedy show, so I had to write *'I'm lovely, all I am is lovely, lovely is the one thing I can do.'* Well, Eydie Gorme is just not going to sing a song that says *'Lovely is the one thing I can do,'* is she? So I screwed myself out of a possible hit."[44]

Alan Jay Lerner found a solution of sorts to this problem by confining the more show-specific elements to the verse (often omitted in cover versions), leaving the chorus with a more broadly generic lyric, e.g. "I've Grown Accustomed to Her Face" and, to a lesser extent, "Almost Like Being in Love". In the so-called Golden Age, hit songs occasionally even came from flop musicals, such as "The Gentleman is a Dope" (from Rodgers and Hammerstein's *Allegro*) and the title song from Lerner and Burton Lane's *On a Clear Day You Can See Forever*.

However, composer Alan Menkin says, "If a show has a clear and marketable concept, with enough structural integrity and production values to deliver

---

[44] P. Max Wilk, *They're Playing Our Song*, Atheneum, New York, 1973, 236-7

on that concept, the quality of the songwriting is not the principal concern. Songs, although the driving force of a musical-theater piece, are perceived and commented on, based more on their style and intent, rather than their intrinsic quality. That's not to say that quality of songwriting has actually diminished. But great songs are not an absolute necessity for a show to succeed."[45] Really?

"I tend to agree with Alan Menkin", says John Sparks. "Not that great songs aren't needed – they are! But not necessarily great in the chart-topping or even 'take-home-hummable' sense… Writers… need to concentrate on dramaturgy – tell the story, who does what to whom, why and what is riding on the outcome of the action."

Menkin's point may be an accurate observation, but does it bode well for the future of the musical? Have musical writers become so obsessed with dramaturgy that they have – musically at least – lost the plot? I hear audiences complain that modern Broadway musicals have no memorable songs, and so they turn to revivals and jukebox musicals. Is it too much to ask that songs be both functional and memorable? Frank Loesser managed it many, many times. So did Rodgers and Hammerstein. *Carousel* is full of songs that advance the dramaturgy yet have become standards.

---

[45] " How Can Musical Theater Be Saved? Broadway Veterans Give Their Advice", Scott Brown,, Vulture.com 24 May 2012

Lyricist Tom Jones (*The Fantasticks*) says, "Partly in rebellion against the long established (and too easily anticipated) [Rodgers and Hammerstein] format, there is a desire to make musicals less simple and more challenging, not only in their songs, but in their stories and characters. I personally think this is a good thing. If the musical is ever to 'grow up' and become more than just a happy-go-lucky reassuring pop massage, it must be able to take on stories or characters that are more complex. And it must be able to bring them to life in song forms that are more flexible than the old thirty-two bar AABA. There must be room for recitative, for long-line and diffuse musical elements. Having said that, I hasten to add that these complexities must not replace the popular song form, but be an addition to it... Blocks of music built around one basic, simple, solid *song* with a memorable melody and a clear lyric." [46]

I would argue that if "What I Did for Love" is weak, it's because Kleban assumed that a "hit" song had to have a generic lyric. The problem with that song is that it just doesn't sound like something that a character would say. I believe that he could have come up with a way of expressing the same sentiment in words that sound like they came out of the mouth of Diana Morales, and still have had a memorable "take home tune". What did she do for love? What sacrifices did she make to be a dancer? The song doesn't tell us that. It seems ironic given that so many

---

[46] Tom Jones, *Making Musicals*, Limelight Editions, New York, 1998,p. 134-139.

of the popular songs of the past fifty years have come from singer-songwriters expressing what is very personal to them that anybody should think a hit show tune has to be generic. If the world can accept Joni Mitchell pouring her heart out, surely it can accept Diana Morales – a fictional character – doing the same.

I find it hard to imagine that a century ago, people found the music of Debussy and Satie (among others) to be dissonant, as to my ears it is lushly harmonic. However, they achieved this by contrasting the harmony against dissonance, thus highlighting it. In a similar vein, in the song "God That's Good!" in *Sweeney Todd*, Stephen Sondheim allows the rich, almost romantic melody ("Is that a pie fit for a king?...") to rise up out of the cacophony. The fact that this rhapsodic melody is accompanied by a lyric referring to cannibalism and murder simply piles on the irony. The lesson is that, just as darkness can be used to point to the light, the discord helps you to hear the melody; it is not there for its own sake.

In opera (as well as in film scores), a leitmotif is a theme that is used as an icon, a kind of musical signpost. Grove's Dictionary of Music defines a leitmotif as "a theme, or other coherent idea, clearly defined so as to retain its identity if modified on subsequent appearances, and whose purpose is to represent or symbolise a person, object, place, idea, state of mind, supernatural force or any other ingredient in a dramatic work, usually operatic but also vocal, choral or instrumental".[47] In a musical, leitmotifs are a form of mnemonic that helps the audience to remember and recognise key plot points in a story. What is the point of a leitmotif if one doesn't recognise its recurrence? Is not the same principle true of a song? How can we expect a song to be effective if it's not memorable?

Los Angeles based producer and lyricist Mitchell Glaser says, "What are actually needed are stand-out moments, and the best moment in a musical had better include a song or you are doing something wrong in my opinion." I know that when I begin work on a musical score, I like to find the emotional core of the piece and start from there. That song may or may not end up being the "big number" that the show is identified with, but it will likely be a song of yearning.

Placement is everything. Many a good song is lost because it's in a place that doesn't deserve it, or where its characters haven't earned the right to sing. It is at this point that the audience collectively rolls its eyes and exclaims, "Not another bloody song!" Bearing this in mind, "What I Did for Love" holds the classic "eleven o'clock" position in *A Chorus Line*, and its basic sentiment strikes at the heart of what the show is all about. It's true that its lyrics could have been made more character based, but I believe this could

---

[47] Arnold Whittall, "Leitmotif." In *Grove Music Online Oxford Music Online* , http://0-www.oxfordmusiconline.com.catalog.lib.cmich.edu:80/subscriber/article/grove/music/16360

have been done without losing its viability outside of the show.

Stephen Oles makes an interesting point when he talks about emotion in theatre songs. I remember having a discussion with a fellow lyricist – the creator of somewhat campy kitsch shows – in which she told me that she would never write about anything she was emotionally invested in – how else would she maintain detachment? While for many people the best remembered song in *Wicked* is probably "Defying Gravity", for me it is "I'm not that Girl", a song that expresses its character's deep vulnerability. It's not afraid of emotion, nor is it a mawkish "power ballad". I believe that's because Stephen Schwartz was not afraid to invest himself in that song. (He once told me that he regarded his work on *The Baker's Wife* as a sort of Freudian therapy session.) While *Wicked*'s score certainly does contain power ballads, it was this tender and restrained number that for me touched the core of the piece.

Among the fraternity of musical theatre writers, it is "politically correct" to worship at the altar of Sondheim, while deriding the mostly European pop operas. I find myself somewhere in the middle. While I think that *Les Misérables* contains some of the feeblest recitative ever written, its big moments certainly come off and connect with a very wide audience, a quality that we ignore to our peril. "A lot of the best work in musicals is happening in small spaces," says London theatre critic Michael Coveney. "What you don't get, and this explains the success of

Jersey Boys… is the discovery of a shared common ground, of a cultural and musical consensus."[48]

I must admit that my beliefs fly in the face of much of what is being taught in musical theatre composition classes, and finding its way onto (usually subsidized or non-profit) stages. When I saw *The Light in the Piazza*, I must confess that the score had no emotional impact on me whatsoever. Even its so-called standout song "Dividing Day" sounded to me like the introduction to a song that never came. (I did not have the same problem with Guettel's earlier work *Floyd Collins* which, although equally musically complex, had a very affecting emotional core.)

"Adam Guettel is a talented guy," says Stephen Oles, "but has he ever written a song anyone but an undergraduate theatre major can love or even remember?" On the other hand, I believe that Guettel's contemporary Michael-John Lachiusa possesses a rhythmic and harmonic inventiveness reminiscent of Leonard Bernstein. To my ears, the music of *Piazza* is dry and brittle. Many people disagree, but the gulf between what the theatre establishment deems to be good and what audiences want to see and hear is widening. I believe that the only way to bridge that gulf is to do what Bernstein (and Mozart) did – to meet them in the middle, and try to entice them our way.

---

[48] Michael Coveney, "Do hit musicals still need great songs?", *The Stage*, London, 22 May 2014, p.10.

Originally published as a blog in October 2013
http://amillionmilesfrombroadway.blogspot.co.uk/2013/10/do-musicals-need-great-songs.html

THE SWEETNESS AND THE SORROW: NATURALISM IN *A CHORUS LINE*

It is commonly presumed that the Broadway musical is a presentational (as opposed to naturalistic) form. Naturalism is defined by Émile Zola as "the return to nature and to man, direct observation, exact anatomy, the acceptance and depicting of what is… No more abstract characters in books, no more lying inventions, no more of the absolute, but real characters, the true history of each one, the story of daily life."[49] In the presentational form, the presence of an audience is, at least implicitly, acknowledged.[50]

---

[49] Emile Zola, "Naturalism on the Stage", *The Experimental Novel and Other Essays*, Cassell Publishing Co., New York, 1894. p. 114
[50] Elam , Keir. 1980. *The Semiotics of Theatre and Drama*. New Accents Ser. Methuen _p.90-91.

Naturalism eschews romanticism and depictions of the metaphysical, aiming instead for behaviouristic settings and characters. Musicals, with their roots in vaudeville, are thought to be largely escapist, and thereby hardly a depiction of "what is". For the purpose of this essay, rather than enter into a general discussion of naturalism vs. theatricality in a musical, I have chosen to focus exclusively on one show that attempts to use the two forms side by side.

Although *A Chorus Line* is a glitzy Broadway musical with all the artifice of a Las Vegas revue, it also contains elements that suggest naturalism in a way that is unusual in the musical theatre. In fact, it shares many of the same conceptual techniques as collectively written shows such as *Oh! What a Lovely War* and even the "verbatim" musical *London Road*. In its original production, the show was set in an un-named Broadway theatre in the present, and took place in real time, in what would appear to be an attempt to combine naturalism with performance into a kind of documentary theatre. However, the style of acting and delivery is often at odds with the naturalism and realism of its setting and conception.

One night in 1974, dancers Michon Peacock and Tony Stevens (the latter of whose credits included being assistant choreographer to both Bob Fosse and Gower Champion, and choreographing the film version of *Best Little Whorehouse in Texas*) gathered a group of dancers together at the Nickolaus Exercise Center with a view to forming a new dance company. They were tired of the lack of respect often shown to dancers on Broadway, and they invited director and choreographer Michael Bennett along to bring added gravitas. The three of them wrote out a list of questions to ask each participant: real name, stage name, what his/her childhood was like, etc. Bennett quickly saw the dramatic potential as either a show or a book. "It was the mid-1970s, the era Tom Wolfe labelled the 'Me Decade'", writes one-time cast member Denny Martin Flinn. "Encounter groups and sensitivity sessions and having a shrink were at the height of popularity. Whether they were influenced by the times or the late hour or the shared and similar confidences, the dancers slowly opened up and talked about their lives."[51] The resulting twenty hours of recordings of dancers pouring their hearts out eventually became the basis for *A Chorus Line*. [52]

Bennett then asked one of the participants, dancer Nicholas Dante, to begin the process of turning the material into a script. Dante used his own experience to create the character of Paul, who recalls the night his parents saw him perform in a drag act. "I was afraid to tell my story", he told *Newsday* in 1975; "my story was Paul's story," he said. "But I felt that if I was going to help the evening, then I had to open up. I did, and I told my story, which was devastating to

---

[51] Flinn, Denny Martin, *What They Did for Love – The Untold Story Behind the Making of A CHORUS LINE*, Bantam Books, New York, 1989, p.31.
[52] Mandelbaum, Ken, *A Chorus Line and the Musicals of Michael Bennett*. St. Martins Press, New York, 1990. ISBN 0-312-03061-4. ,p 108.

Michael and to a lot of people." [53] This monologue was the only one that survived into the final script in more-or-less unaltered form.

Of the original workshop participants, eight would go on to play in the original production – although they each had to audition for their own part. (Some of the remaining participants, including Dante, would later join the replacement casts.) However, not all were playing themselves – Donna McKechnie would play a newly invented character named Cassie, while another actress was introduced to play Maggie, the part based on McKechnie's early experiences.

Author and playwright James Kirkwood Jr. was later brought in to give the script some sense of structure. "There has always been a controversy about those tapes", Kirkwood told a panel of librettists in 1985. "Ed Kleban, who was in on the project before I was, knows that I never heard those tapes. Michael played me about five minutes of them one time just to get the sound of all those people talking. I defy you to get twenty-some dancers in a room and have them talk together and get a lot from them. I mean, I did get a transcript of it, but what you get from that is some characters, and you get a diversity of personalities to pick up on, but then the writer had to put that together." [54] Of the creative team (Nicholas Dante and James Kirkwood, book; Ed Kleban, lyrics and

[53] "Nicholas Dante; 'Chorus Line' Co-Author", *Los Angeles Times*, 22 May 1991.
[54] Guernsey, Otis L.; McNally, Terrence (eds.) *Broadway Song and Story – Playwrights, Lyricists Composers Discuss Their Hits*, Dodd Mead, 1985.

Marvin Hamlisch, music) only Kleban, a student of the BMI Musical Theatre Workshops, had ever written a musical before.

The following is an extract from the original workshop tapes in which actress Priscilla Lopez, on whom the character of Diana Morales was based, relates the story that would eventually become the song "Nothing":

> The first day of acting class, they put us down on the stage and it was like, 'okay, we're going to do improvisation'. Improvisation? What's an improvisation? So he puts us on the floor, one in back of the other with our legs like this around everybody, 'Okay now, you're skiing – no, you're on a bobsled. It's snowing out. Okay, go!' I'm standing there thinking, what am I doing? What am I doing? Until finally the three minutes are up for improvisation, and he says, 'Okay, now what did you feel?' Hands started to shoot up – I felt the snow, I felt the rain, I felt the cold. 'What did you feel?' I didn't feel anything! Well, that was it. I slit my throat, and it was the first day of school. It was terrible... They are so destructive in that school because they let children who know nothing about anything criticize other children. And usually the criticism is just to satisfy

what they think the teacher wants to hear anyway. So they knew I wasn't on his good side so any time I got up there I'd be completely – I couldn't do anything right! … Anyway, he wanted me to leave the school. I told him I'd have to go to Girls High if I left, and that was really the worst. So he said, 'Well, I think there's a little spark there, and maybe something will happen.' And I thought, if there's this little spark and you make me leave the school, then how is this little spark – and I did miserably the rest of the year and I was unhappy, and then that summer he died. And I'm telling you, I was so happy. I didn't want him to die, but only because I felt this weight just lifted off my shoulder and it was better. [55]

Compare this to what was spoken and sung in the final show: "I'm so excited because I'm going to go to the High School of the Performing Arts. I mean, I was dying to be a serious actress. Anyway, it's the first day of acting class and we're in the auditorium and the teacher Mr. Karp" – the teacher was given a name – "puts us up on the stage with our legs around everybody, one in back of the other and he says, 'Okay, we're going to do improvisation. Now, you're on a bobsled and

---

[55] Adam de Dio, James D. Stern, *Every Little Step* (film), Endgame Entertainment, 2008. (DVD bonus feature)

it's snowing out, and it's cold. Okay, go'." At this point, Ed Kleban the lyricist takes over: "Every day for a week we would try to feel the motion, feel the motion, down the hill. Every day for a week we would try to hear the wind rush, hear the wind rush, feel the chill. And I dug right down to the bottom of my soul to see what I had inside. Yes I dug right down to the bottom of my soul and I tried, I tried". Then it switches back to dialogue: "And everybody's going [woosh, woosh] I feel the snow, I feel the cold, I feel the air, and Mr. Karp turns to me and he says, 'Okay Morales, what did you feel?' Then the song takes over again: "And I said 'Nothing, I'm feeling nothing', and he said 'Nothing would get a girl transferred.' They all felt something, but I felt nothing, except the feeling that this bullshit was absurd." Priscilla Lopez's complaint about the children's criticism became the lyric "The kids yelled 'nothing!' They called me nothing, and Karp allowed it, which really makes me burn. They were so helpful — They called me 'hopeless', until I really didn't know where else to turn". Finally, the song ends with "Six months later I heard that Karp had died, and I dug right down to the bottom of my soul and cried — 'cause I felt nothing".[56] All of the important story elements were retained, and a few

---

[56] Nicholas Dante, James Kirkwood (book), Ed Kleban (lyrics), *A Chorus Line*, 1975.

phrases were taken verbatim, but it was focused and given a rhythm.

The original pretence that the audience is a fly-on-the-wall watching a real Broadway audition was abandoned after a few years. As Bud Coffey, Production Stage Manager for the International Company of *A Chorus Line* explained to me in 1982, "We recently changed the date to 1975, because they had been updating it, and they felt that we were far enough away from '75 that it should become a period piece. We couldn't keep updating all the little things in the show – names, references, things like that – so they decided to go back to 1975, and the show works much better without trying to update... It's more of the seventies than of the eighties."[57]

The show begins realistically enough on a bare stage. The music is, at first, diagetic as Larry the dance captain puts a group of dancers through their paces. As the musical prologue segues into the song "I Hope I Get It", it becomes more like a conventional book musical. Then, as the individual characters are introduced, their monologues often feel more like stand-up comedy routines – especially in the cases of Bobby, Sheila, Greg and Val. (Some of these routines were, in fact, ghost-written by playwright Neil Simon.)

---

[57] Interview with the author, 19 August 1982.

Although the parts are based on real speeches – often made by the same people now performing them as "characters" – they assume an air of artifice, largely because of a broad, bigger-than-life acting style. Of course, this "artifice" may exist in real life – even Zach (the director's) comments suggests he wishes they would stop "performing".

The show's finale number, "One" also begins as a diagetic number, with the dance captain teaching the steps to the dancers, accompanied by a rehearsal pianist. As the orchestra comes in, it makes its transition to becoming presentational. Perhaps it was Michael Bennett's intention to contrast the dancer's real lives with this escapist fantasy. It is also a deconstruction of a classic Broadway promenade: in its first iteration, it lifts the veil on its own artifice, allowing the audience to see the sweat that has gone into its creation. Even some of the presentational aspects of the show are seen as naturalistic when presented in a diagetic form. Only the presence of an orchestra and stage lighting breaks this illusion.

A *Chorus Line* aims for an unprecedented level of naturalism in its depiction of the lives of its dancer-characters, based on the real-life experiences of its workshop participants. Whether or not the naturalism is compromised by the presentational aspects depends to some extent on how one defines naturalism. If one accepts the notion of song and dance numbers merely as an entertaining diversion for the tired Manhattan businessman, then this may be the case. However, if one sees in its songs an "inside track" into the feelings and aspirations of its characters, then one could argue that it achieves a form of realism that goes beyond Ibsen and Strindberg.

I have seen four different Broadway touring productions of *A Chorus Line*, all in the late seventies/early eighties. In the first (ca 1978), the references were updated, and the setting was indicated as "the present". In all of the others, it had been frozen to 1975. In each case, as well as in the 1985 film version, I felt that the naturalism had been diminished – not by the musical theatre elements, but by the broad, shout-it-to-the-rafters acting style, especially when delivering those Neil Simon-provided one-liners. On stage, it may be that a subtle, naturalistic form doesn't work in the large musical houses that *A Chorus Line* must, by economic necessity, play in. Some have noted that this element of the show changed when it moved from the 300 seat Public Theatre to the Shubert on Broadway. Original actor Don Percassi observed, "It became a Broadway show. It became a different show. It became a commercial show. There's one thing Michael taught me. He said, 'It's show *business*, not *show* business."[58]

Thus, my contention is that while the act of performing may not render the naturalistic musical a contradiction in terms per se, in this case it makes for a sometimes awkward coexistence. Would a more subtle, naturalistic acting style mitigate this problem? Given the show's scale and economics, we may never know.

Originally written as an essay in the MA in Musical Theatre program at Goldsmiths University of London, 2015.

---

[58] Flinn, p.150.

The Beginnings of *Evita*

Perhaps it is significant that the studio where the original concept album of *Evita* was recorded began its "life" as a live theatre. In the 1920s, what was then known as the Barnes Theatre was the venue for some of the earliest appearances of John Gielgud and Charles Laughton. It later went through periods as a cinema and television studio before becoming the home of Olympic Sound in 1966. *Evita*, which was recorded there in 1976, would make the reverse transition – from record album to stage production to film. How was this transition made, and to what extent does the finished product betray its concept album roots?

Firstly, let's look at how its initial structure was arrived at. Six years earlier, in the same studio, Andrew Lloyd Webber and Tim Rice had produced *Jesus Christ Superstar* as a concept album because they lacked the theatrical connections and clout to bring it directly to the stage.[59] Calling it a "rock opera", it followed quickly on the heels of The Who's 1969 album *Tommy*, and managed to gain "street cred" in pop music circles by featuring Deep Purple's lead singer Ian Gillan in the role of Jesus as well as members of Joe Cocker's Grease Band, even though its creators were influenced by Rodgers and

---

[59] Tim Rice, *What a Circus*, Hodder and Stoughton, London, 1999, p 342.

Hammerstein[60] as much as by Lennon and McCartney.

However, with *Evita*, they chose deliberately to make the album first, believing that they could then establish whether or not the underlying material worked before adding other theatrical elements. As Tim Rice says, "There are so many things that can go wrong with a stage musical that the writers of the score of a flop can never be really sure whether they were to blame."[61] This was not a new idea; as early as 1954, *Archy and Mehitabel* with music by George Kleinsinger and lyrics by Joe Darion based on Don Marquis's *New York Tribune* columns was released as a concept album starring Carol Channing and Eddie Bracken. This was adapted for the stage in a 1957 Broadway production re-titled *Shinbone Alley* featuring Eartha Kitt and with a book by Mel Brooks. Similarly, *You're a Good Man, Charlie Brown* was originally produced as a record in 1966, with Orson Bean in the title role. The off-Broadway stage version opened the following year.

Although the initial inspiration for the concept album of *Evita* came from a BBC radio program about Eva Perón called *Legends in our Lifetime*, it was Carlos Pasini's 1972 Thames TV documentary *Queen of Hearts* that gave Rice the foundation for his work. (Pasini would contribute his voice to the original concept

---

[60] Jonathan Mantle, *Fanfare: The Unauthorised Biography of Andrew Lloyd Webber*, Michael Joseph Ltd., London, 1989, p10.
[61] Tim Rice, *Evita – The Legend of EVA PERON*, Avon Books, New York, 1978. (No page numbers)

album as one of the Spanish-speaking actors in the phoney movie that is heard in the opening sequence, as well as the voice announcing the death of Evita, and also provided the archive photos for the album package.) Some newsreel shots included crowds chanting "Peron! Peron! Peron!" The film even "inspired" one of the tunes – Lloyd Webber lifted the melody for "The Money Kept Rolling In" more or less intact from a Perónist marching song heard over the end titles.[62]

Rice began sketching out the synopsis for *Evita* early in 1974. Lloyd Webber was not yet on board as composer, as he was committed to the ill-fated musical *Jeeves* with collaborator Alan Ayckbourn. (Rice had already wisely bailed as lyricist on this latter venture.)

In *Jesus Christ Superstar*, Rice had used the character of Judas Iscariot as an antagonistic narrator. At first, Rice proposed to tell the story of Evita in a similar fashion through the eyes of a hairdresser named "Mario". (Eva's real-life hairdresser had featured in Pasini's film.)

Then he realised that Ernesto "Che" Guevara had been born in Argentina. "I thought: 'Hang on – Che would be much more interesting than some unknown hairdresser. That way, I get two icons for the price of one.'"[63] Anybody who has read or seen the film of

---

[62] Rice, p. 371
[63] Laura Barnett, "How we made Evita: Tim Rice and Elaine Paige", *The Guardian*, 9 September 2014.

Guevara's *Motorcycle Diaries* will know that the poverty he witnessed en route was the cause of his disenchantment, but Rice preferred to dwell on an early and little-known attempt by Guevara at free enterprise. In 1950 he had patented an insecticide, initially calling it "Al Capone", (until he was told he would require the permission of the gangster's family). He then considered calling it "Atilla the Hun" since it would kill everything in its path, but finally settled on the name Vendaval, which means "Hurricane".[64]

Like Lloyd Webber, Rice is a life-long Conservative and was amused by the revolutionary leader's early brush with capitalism. He proposed that Che became disillusioned with Perónism partly because of his own business failure, in order to "suggest that Che and Eva were really cut from the same grasping cloth." [65] This became a rather bizarre sidebar to the plot on the concept album, but since Che was at this point never explicitly identified as Guevara, it made little sense to the audience, and seemed to pull focus from the main story. "This mischievous viewpoint was referred to at odd points during the original album of *Evita*," says Rice, "but disappeared at the request of just about everyone in subsequent versions." [66]

---

[64] John Lee Anderson, *Che Guevara: A Revolutionary Life*, Bantam Press, London, 1997, p. 57
[65] Rice, P. 358.
[66] Op. cit.

As it turns out, *Evita* would change far more on its way to the stage than *Superstar* did. While the published libretto suggests that Rice always broadly envisioned this as a stage work, with every song having a dramatic context, there is little evidence that he had worked out the scenography in any detail. A concept album is similar to a radio play in that, being an audio medium, all major exposition must come through the aural senses. *Jesus Christ Superstar* presented a simple story already familiar to most of its audience. For *Evita*, a history lesson was necessary. Thus, through the character of Che, we were given narrative songs such as "The Lady's Got Potential" (cut from the stage version but reinstated with revised lyrics in the film). It told of Perón's military background and the formation of the G.O.U. ("Grupo de Oficiales Unidos") a secret society that would soon form a military coup. The problem is, it described the events, rather than showing them. This would be replaced on stage by "The Art of the Possible", in which the generals are shown in a game of musical chairs. The difference is striking: the latter was, both musically and lyrically, tailored to fit into director Harold Prince's scenic concept.

Of course, it is not just the libretto that tells the story. As the composer says, "What fascinates me most is the way that music can cut corners and say something quite quickly that it would take far longer to say in words."[67] He cites the key modulation in "Eva Beware of the City" to indicate that she got her way and went to Buenos Aires against Migaldi's advice.

---

[67] Rice, *Evita – The Legend of EVA PERON*, no page number given.

The album was accompanied by a booklet illustrated with photographs of the real Peróns (courtesy of Carlos Pasini) in addition to a full libretto and plot synopsis. Rice even wrote a book called *Evita: The Legend of Eva Perón (1919-1952)* published by Elm Tree Books in 1978 to coincide with the London opening of the stage version. This shows how anxious he was to familiarise the audience with the historical details without cluttering the plot with them. In the work itself, most of the back-story and political subtext is revealed in direct exposition by the character of Che, but Rice's idea of making Che a fly-killing mogul considerably muddied the plot, and it's easy to see why he was prevailed upon to change it.

Once the album was finished, Lloyd Webber sent it to Harold Prince. "When they sent me the lyrics for *Evita*, I wrote a three thousand word response about how to transform a group of songs into a dramatic script with tension", Prince says.[68] In this response, he wrote "I had a feeling (which grew) that something is missing in the second act. [In the original outline, the first act ends with "Don't Cry For Me, Argentina", although the actual break between discs is at the end of "A New Argentina", which is where the interval falls in the stage version.] That *fate* intervenes and levels Evita rather than instruments of her own doing. You touch on growing disillusionment within the government, but you don't describe it theatrically.

---

[68] Foster Hirsch, *Harold Prince and the American Musical Theatre*, Applause Theatre and Cinema Books, New York, 1989, p. 159.

There is no confrontation in which Evita (and Perón) accelerate their own downfall."[69]

Prince later gave them a complete dramatic breakdown. "I created a script from lyrics by always looking for points of conflict such as Evita's single-mindedness vs. Perón's cowardice – he would have quit if she hadn't been pushing, and that kind of pulling is terrific in the theatre. That central conflict together with the Cinderella story of Evita's rise from poverty to power is very seductive."[70] He asked Rice to add a couple of short expository monologues for Che, including one in the second act in which he rails against the economic ruin wrought by Perón.
In his initial critique, Prince thought Che was too British. "I think some of his recitative is corny, quite frankly below the rest of the material. I don't get a clear character as I do Eva and Perón and some of the minor characters. He seems a rock performer. 'Listen chum, face the fact, they don't like your act' and 'Which means get stuffed' also seem too British."[71] Prince was also reluctant to premiere the show in London, which he felt "clung too tenaciously to rigid demarcation lines between operetta and musical theatre"[72]. To the rock opera counter-culture he may have seemed "old-Broadway", but all of his shows from *Cabaret* (1966) on had defied convention. Before the London opening, Lloyd Webber said "I hope that, particularly with the guidance of Hal Prince, the

---

[69] Rice, p. 386.

[70] Hirsch, p. 159.

[71] Rice, p. 387.

[72] Gerald McKnight, *Andrew Lloyd Webber – A biography*, Granada, London, 1984, p.175

revised version which will be staged will add new dimensions and clarify much that was not immediately obvious on record. There was incidentally quite a bit of material that had to be cut from the first recordings because of the length. Our hope is that *Evita* in the theatre will become a specifically theatrical piece that has benefited from the recording studio rather than just being a product of it."[73]

One of the biggest changes in the theatrical version was the sound of the music, which Prince had re-orchestrated by Hershy Kay (1919-81), with whom he had worked on *On the Twentieth Century*. The Latin rhythms were accentuated, but the rock elements softened.

The failure of *Jeeves* in 1975 had, Lloyd Webber believed, taught him a number of lessons. The first was never to work beyond his level of expertise. The second was to work only with collaborators who understood musical theatre. The third was never to begin rehearsals without a workable script. The fourth was to control as many aspects of the production himself as he could. The fifth was never again to write a book musical – the music must be the driving force. In this author's opinion, the last two may have been the wrong lessons. Ever since *Phantom of the Opera*, he has acted as his own producer (through his Really Useful Group) which has made him so powerful that nobody can warn him when he is going off the rails. This has not improved

---

[73] Rice, *Legend*, no page number given.

his success rate, nor did it prevent him from having flops like *Whistle Down the Wind* and *Stephen Ward* (to name only two). And, in fact, most of his work since *Phantom of the Opera* has contained at least some spoken dialogue.

The original recording of *Evita* produced a major hit single, but not the one its creators were expecting. "Another Suitcase in Another Hall" had been earmarked as a potential hit, but it was the song that was originally titled "It's Only Your Lover Returning" that eventually triumphed. It finally became "Don't Cry For Me, Argentina", a title drawn from Evita's actual epitaph on her tomb in Buenos Aires' Recoleta cemetery.

"Rice's first draft had been largely factual and biographical", says biographer Michael Walsh, "but Lloyd Webber insisted that a mere retelling of Eva's rise and fall was not enough. For *Evita* to work it needed a hook – a dominant idea that would crystallize the whole show into a few minutes of overwhelming emotional power."[74] Lloyd Webber's inspiration for this came from having seen Judy Garland perform at a London cabaret toward the end of her life. Her performance of "Over the Rainbow" was a pale impression of herself. Her own destruction was seen through her signature song. "And that", says the composer, "was the genesis of

---

[74] Michael Walsh, *Andrew Lloyd Webber – His Life and Works* Harry N. Abrams Inc., New York, 1997, p. 97.

how I felt we should make the big song work."[75]
"The tone was deliberately banal", says critic Michael
Coveney, "as in a Hollywood Oscar acceptance
speech, and the first point was that Eva was being
deliberately insincere, seducing the audience with
more style than content."[76] "The irony is that she was
conning people without them realising what she was
saying", says Tim Rice. "Which is precisely what
happened with a mega hit with people who had no
idea it was part of a show. In a way, it proved we'd
got it right."[77] Against all odds, the song became a
million-selling hit single, in spite of its length and lack
of a danceable beat.

Having a successful concept album ahead of a show's
opening can be a mixed blessing. Audiences will
expect to see on stage what they heard on record.
When a song becomes familiar to the public, it is
tempting to keep it even if it is no longer working
within the show. But, as *Chess* later demonstrated, a
successful concept album is no guarantee of theatrical
success. Stacking the deck in the authors' favour may
not, in the long run, be a good thing if it inhibits the
director from solving structural problems.

"We were working from a record album with no real
book", says choreographer Larry Fuller. "Hal took
those lyrics and made a show, a documentary in
revue form. We picked a new image – a new visual

---

[75] Michael Coveney, *The Andrew Lloyd Webber Story*, Arrow Books,
London, 1999, p. 98.
[76] Coveney, pp 98-9
[77] Op cit, p. 100.

metaphor – for each number, and we couldn't repeat or mix the metaphors."[78] Confronted with the challenge of how to depict a political rally with a relatively small cast, Prince populated the stage with political campaign graphics, giving the illusion of the masses. He was imposing visuals on a piece that was largely conceived for audio.

"The show succeeds despite breaking one of the cardinal rules of the theatre – to *show* action, instead of describing it," says Scott Miller, artistic director of New Line Theatre in St. Louis, Missouri, who presented *Evita* in 2010. "So much of *Evita* is narration that some labelled it an oratorio rather than a musical or opera. But this story must exist primarily as narration, because the central conflict of the story is the real-life conflict between the two surviving narratives of Eva's life and career."[79]

In considering the question of how *Evita* betrays its origins as a concept album, let's look at how that central conflict between Eva and Che is structured. In fact, it is entirely invented: the two characters paths never crossed in real life. Her other major conflict was with the generals, but they are treated as a chorus, a sort-of mass character with no individual identities. Perón himself is defined only by his relationship with Eva. We never actually see Perón do anything, or express any political ideas except as

[78] Hirsch, p. 165.
[79] Scott Miller, *Inside Evita: Background and Analysis*, http://www.newlinetheatre.com/evitachapter.html Accessed 25 April 2015.

they relate to her. The conflict is more of ideas than of actions. Che tells us that Perón is evil, but we are never really allowed to see a tyrant in action.

"We're used to believing the narrator in a show or novel", says Scott Miller. "But like the Leading Player in *Pippin* and the Balladeer in *Assassins*, Che is a narrator with an agenda. He can lie. He is hardly impartial. We soon realize that we're getting two diametrically opposed points of view in *Evita*. Can we know that Che's accusations are true? We see no evidence that Eva stole money from her foundation (in real life, Juan Perón did most of the dirty work). And if the poor are so much worse off, as Che claims, then why do they love Eva and Juan so much? Maybe no one on stage is telling the whole truth, including Che as narrator... Perhaps Che and Eva cannot find common ground because he comes from a position of political philosophy and she comes from a position of emotion."[80]

"The New York production was tricky," says Rice. "It won Tony awards, but we got bad reviews from critics saying it was a fascist play, which was just ludicrous."[81] On the other hand, a review by Quentin Letts of the 2014 UK touring production in the right-leaning *Daily Mail* seems to equate the Peróns with the British left – especially Scottish nationalists. "Does the example of Juan Peron in Argentina in the 1940s and 50s not show us the limits of nationalism?

---

[80] Miller, loc. Cit.
[81] Barnett, loc. cit.

Peron, lent glamour and mass-market protection by his singer [sic] wife, was a plausible liberator. He appealed to narrow, simplistic patriotism, sprinkling favours he could not afford on a people who would later pay the economic price. He and his wife resented Press critics. They plotted against the middle classes. They created division. Remind you of anyone?"[82]

If the politics of *Evita* seem to be a bit confused, it may be partly because although Lloyd Webber and Rice are self-described conservatives, Prince certainly is not, and neither is Alan Parker, director of the film version. Jean Graham-Jones, Associate Professor of Theatre at CUNY's Graduate Center and Hunter College and author of *Exorcising History: Argentine Theater under Dictatorship* observes "*Evita*'s oversimplified dismissal of Perónism as simply "common or garden fascism" (Rice's phrase), with no understanding of or appreciation for the complexities of Perón's Justicialist Party, a political movement that included factions from the Right, the Center, and the Left."[83] Pablo Gorlero, critic for *La Nación*, a conservative Buenos Aires newspaper, says "We considered Lloyd Webber's *Evita* as a fake history." According to him, when Tim Rice came to Buenos Aires, he spoke only to the upper class people who

---

[82] *Daily Mail*, London, 23 September 2014.
[83] Jean Graham-Jones, "' The truth is… My Soul is With You': Documenting a Tale of Two Evitas", Theatre Survey, May 2005, p. 76.

hated Perónism. "He didn't [do any] historical research about Evita."[84]

Rice left it for the audience to decide whether Eva was good or bad, although he clearly meant it as a cautionary tale. So what about Prince's criticisms? Was the problem he identified in Act Two solved? While it is clear that, as Rice says, "the knives are out", it was Eva's illness and not the generals' plotting that brought her life on top to an end. Prince cut "Eva's Sonnet" down to just six lines. (In the film, it was eliminated entirely, and replaced by a new song, "You Must Love Me". In musical theatre, emotion trumps intellectual discourse every time.) "The Money Kept Rolling In" was made even more cynical by suggesting that the Peróns kept Swiss bank accounts. But on stage, while it may have been inevitable that had she lived they would have been overthrown – as Juan Perón was just three years later – Rice's structure remained largely intact. Her immortality/martyrdom was guaranteed, enhanced by Prince's revelation that her body disappeared for seventeen years. (As I write this, another film drama, *Eva Doesn't Sleep* is in the works that will tell of this disappearance.)

In 1996, *Evita* went through another transformation when Alan Parker directed a film version, with a screenplay by Oliver Stone. Although the film in some ways returned to the concept album, its "show,

---

[84] Mel Atkey, *A Million Miles from Broadway -- Musical Theatre Beyond New York and London*, Friendlysong Books, Vancouver, p. 194.

don't tell" ethos – in this writer's opinion – solved some of the structural problems in a way the stage version never could. In the film, we actually see the violence of Argentina's civil war. Parker and Stone filled in many of the background details – we saw young Eva being spurned at her father's funeral, rather than just having it described. Most importantly, her beloved descamisados – the "shirtless ones" – were there up on screen, and their reactions to her death are somehow more potent.

The 2006 London revival of *Evita* included some of the revisions made for the film, including the song "You Must Love Me", and Che was returned to his more ambiguous "everyman" role, as in the concept album. It may be that Lloyd Webber and Rice's decision to premier the piece on record as a "proof of concept" to bolster the integrity of their original conception has in fact resulted in a work that is neither fish nor fowl. It was neither conceived specifically as a piece to fit the "empty space" nor as a purely aural experience. It is somewhere in between.

This was originally written as an essay for my MA in Musical Theatre at Goldsmiths, 2016.

Harold Prince or Bob Fosse:
Who Would You Rather Have Direct Your Musical?

I remember, very early in my career, having a telephone conversation with Stephen Schwartz about the director Harold Prince, with whom he would like to have worked on Pippin, and Bob Fosse, the noted director-choreographer with whom he actually did the show. One likes to put his personal stamp on a show, while the other was, Schwartz believed, more concerned with discovering and incubating the intentions of the piece – finding out what it wants to be.

Harold (Hal) Prince (1928-) and Bob Fosse (1927-87) were two of the most influential directors in the history of the Broadway musical. They both made their Broadway debuts in 1955 with the same show, *The Pajama Game*, which Prince co-produced with George Abbott (1887-1995) and Fosse choreographed. Both worked in other areas for a number of years before turning to directing: Fosse had been a dancer (and occasional choreographer) in Hollywood, where his credits included *Kiss Me Kate* and *My Sister Eileen*. Prince, who had worked as a stage manager under his mentor, the aforementioned Abbott, would produce *West Side Story* and *Fiddler on the Roof* before his first major success as a director, *Cabaret*.

Neither director was formally trained in the conventional sense, although Fosse did study acting with Sanford Meisner (1905-97). Both were mentored by Abbott, a man whose own career as a director, writer and producer lasted nearly a century.

Book writer Peter Stone once told me that what interested Fosse was the life that exists under rocks and logs. In other words, the underbelly of humanity – the decadence as reflected in *Chicago*, *Sweet Charity* and *Cabaret*.

In *Pajama Game*, Fosse established what became known as the Fosse style with "Steam Heat". Danced originally by Carol Haney, Buzz Miller and Peter Generro (himself a future choreographer), the number contains several examples of what would become Fosse trademarks. One of these is the use of sound effects (both musical and vocal) that were a carry-over from the slap-stick "rim-shots" he had known as a vaudeville dancer. In this number, the knocks and hisses of a radiator are suggested. His use of black bowler hats also harkens to vaudeville and silent movies. According to Fosse dancer Ann Reinking (1949-), "He very much liked the use of tacit, or silent, count, where nothing is happening. He also liked percussion. His is a world of angular movement and mystery, quiet, semi-taciturn and percussive."[85] Debra McWaters, Artistic Director of the Broadway Theatre Project says that "in some of Fosse's darkest choreography in the 1970s – for his narrator in *Pippin*, his vamps in *Chicago*, his cavorting female band in the film of *Cabaret* – one glimpses

---

[85] Cited in Debra McWaters, *The Fosse Style*, University Press of Florida, Gainsville, FL,2008, p. xiii

German Expressionist antecedents."[86] She adds, "Finally, Charlie Chaplin's Little Tramp is also part of the Fosse style. Fosse admired Chaplin, perhaps more, even, than he admired Fred Astaire, and his friends and colleagues have noted the Chaplinesque aspect of the derby hats, the white gloves, the canes, and the combination of short-gaited walks and vulnerable personalities in many of Fosse's dancing figures." [87] This combo was first found, says former Ballet Russes de Monte Carlo dancer Margery Beddow (1937-2010), in his show-stopping "Steam Heat" trio from *The Pajama Game* of 1956. "This type of trio dance," says Beddow, "with its forward thrust of the hips, hunched shoulders, turned in feet, and sharp, jazzy movements, would become a trademark of his work. Sound effects, derbies, and white gloves were other recurring stylistic elements Fosse first used in this number." [88]

"Steam Heat" was one of the first songs Richard Adler (1921-2012) and Jerry Ross (1926-55) wrote for the show. In fact, it was one of four "audition" songs written on spec to get the job. George Abbott wanted a little number to be performed by what were supposed to be amateurs in a union rally scene. What he did not want was a "show stopper". In fact, he wanted to cut it because it slowed the plot down (which it does), but his directing partner Jerome Robbins prevailed.

---

[86] Loc. Cit.

[87] Vincent Canby, "In a New Vehicle for Bob Fosse, a Joyride of Headlong Energy", *New York Times*, 20 January, 1999.

[88] Margery Beddow, *Bob Fosse's Broadway*, Heinemann, Portsmouth, NH 1996, p. 2.

"When [Carol] Haney sang 'Hernando's Hideaway' to [John] Raitt," Beddow explains, "she used dramatically overdone gestures in the exaggerated style of a vamp from silent films. They arrived at the nightclub in complete darkness; different groups lit matches to direct the audience's attention to each unfolding vignette. Already Fosse was aware of how important lighting was in moving the focus where he wanted it. Throughout his career he continued to make dynamic use of lighting effects. The number also showed his great sense of humor about sexual games. For example, after each dance section, one guy, looking very lost, would wander around in the dark. Holding aloft a lit match, he called out to his girlfriend in a forlorn voice, 'Poopsie... Poopsie!'" "If Charlie Chaplin had been a choreographer", says *New York Times* critic Vincent Canby, "he might have created dances like Fosse's." Except that Fosse did not embrace Chaplin's sentimentality.

Fosse had wanted to make a musical out of Maurine Dallas Watkins' (1896-1969) 1926 play *Chicago*, thinking it would be a good basis for a musical vehicle for his wife, dancer Gwen Verdon (1925-2000), but Watkins, now a born-again Christian, did not believe that a play that glorified a cocktail of murder and showbiz was something she wanted to be attached to. Fosse would have to wait another decade to obtain the rights. In the meantime, somebody suggested that he see the film *Nights of Cabiria* by Federico Fellini. "Most everyone didn't think it was suitable for a musical", says Fosse, "but there were certain things about it that stuck with me, and that night I went home and struggled to go to sleep, and I couldn't. I kept thinking about this movie, so I sat down and wrote like a twelve or fourteen page outline of how I thought it could be made into a musical. I changed it from Italy to New York and made her from a prostitute to a dance hall hostess. I wanted to capture the New York atmosphere with it."[89] He then hired Neil Simon to write the book and Cy Coleman and Dorothy Fields to write the songs for what would become *Sweet Charity*, his debut as a director. However, not all of his projects were based on his own conceptions, and this sometimes led to creative conflicts.

Whereas *Cabaret* (the film), *Chicago* and even *Sweet Charity* were dark subjects, dealing with a seedy milieu, *Pippin*, with music and lyrics by *Godspell* composer Stephen Schwartz (1948-) was, in the beginning, a fairly innocent, folky by-product of the peace and love anti-Viet Nam era. "The thing about doing a show where you're in a sort-of never-never-land time and you have characters who only are relationships and don't really have their own story to tell", says Schwartz, "you can impose almost anything on them. Bob had some feelings of his own and some things he was trying to deal with and I feel that he imposed them on the show for whatever it

---

[89] Dick Strout, interviewer, *Universal Pictures presents "interview specials" and a "feature special" with the stars, composer, director-choreographer and costume designer of the new Motion picture "Sweet Charity"*, 269-USA 1410

was worth, better or worse."[90] Actor John Rubinstein, who played Pippin, said "Stephen was genuinely concerned that his work was being turned into a vaudeville. Bobby was just as genuinely concerned that this sentimental thing was going to have no guts. I thought they were both right." [91] (Interestingly, before Fosse signed on, the show was offered to Hal Prince, who declined, but suggested Schwartz and book writer Roger O. Hirson (1926-) add a second act, which they did.)

This begs the question – why did Fosse choose to direct a show he didn't like? "There's a theory", according to dancer Harvey Evans, "that Fosse picked weaker material so the critics would say 'Oh, it's not much of a show, but what Bob Fosse did with it!'"[92]

There are other theories – that, as a frustrated author, he needed a writer whom he could manipulate. Hirson, whose other Broadway credits included the book for *Walking Happy*, was a veteran of television anthologies from the 1950s.When Schwartz first told Hirson that producer Stuart Ostrow (1932-) had secured Fosse as director, Hirson replied "Yes that's terrific… I just want to tell you that this is our last happy day on the show."[93] To another un-named former collaborator, he was the anti-Christ. (Kander and Ebb had similar problems while working on

[90] Atkey, Mel. *Breaking into Song*, Friendlysong Books, Vancouver, 2015, pp 22-23.
[91] Cited in Martin Gottfried, *All His Jazz – The Life and Death of Bob Fosse* , Da Capo Press, New York, 1990, p.252
[92] Sam Wasson, *Fosse*, Mariner Books, New York, 2013,p.309
[93] Wasson, op cit, p.282.

Chicago. At one point, during the Philadelphia tryouts, Kander said to Ebb, ""Why don't we get on a train and go back to New York. This isn't worth it. No show is worth dying for. Let's go home."[94]) According to Fosse biographer Sam Wasson, Fosse and Ostrow "decided that lampooning the show with anachronistic dialogue and modern attitudes could bring it down to earth, though how they could do it without violating Dramatists Guild regulations, which granted authors script approval, wasn't certain."[95] The answer to the latter question appears to be that, with Ostrow's backing, it was Fosse's way "or the highway".

Once he had hired Ben Vereen for a role originally designated as "Old Man", Fosse set about combining smaller parts to create a sort-of demonic compère called the "Leading Player". This led to the role of Pippin being diminished, and much of the dialogue that gave his character substance was cut. "The character became basically passive and reactive and didn't have the same kind of drive, energy and intelligence that Roger and I were trying to achieve with him", says Schwartz. "Yes, he was innocent, and yes, he was naïve about things, but a lot of specific lines he had got taken away – either given away to the Leading Player or just cut – lines that showed he had a sharp sense of humor or an awareness of what was going on."[96] (Some of these were re-instated in

[94] John Kander, Fred Ebb, Greg Lawrence, *Colored Lights*, Faber and Faber, New York, 2003, p.126

[95] Wasson, loc. cit p.282

[96] Wasson, p. 308

the published script.) In one case, Fosse took what had been a gentle, sincere love song – "With You" – and turned it into a bump and grind orgy. "I don't feel it really works in that context," says Schwartz, "and if I hadn't liked the song so much I probably would have cut it."[97]

"My issue with Bob Fosse", says Schwartz, "was not so much the darkness of his vision but the tawdriness and the emphasis on bumps and grinds and cheap jokes. I also felt that the Leading Player was undercutting the focus on Pippin in some cases and forcing Pippin to become a relatively one-dimensional character."[98] (Again, Kander and Ebb had similar problems on *Chicago*. "Bobby had some really awful stuff that he was putting in the show and we kept wanting him to take it out. It was something really vulgar that distracted from the piece, and we went backstage with all our courage and asked him about it. He got very nasty."[99])

Fosse achieved his famous signature "sound effect" in this show with the song "On the Right Track". According to Schwartz, "When I originally wrote the song, all the notes of the tune had corresponding words. It was Bob's suggestion, in order to provide interesting places for dance and make the song more unusual, that I cut every extraneous word of lyric I could and that he would fill those beats with dance

[97] Atkey, p. 26.

[98] *Pippin - Stephen Schwartz Answers Questions About the Show*, *www.stephenschwartz.com/wp-content/uploads/2010/08/pippin1.pdf*, 2010. Accessed 21 December 2015.

[99] Kander, Ebb & Lawrence, p.125.

steps; this is what led to the idiosyncratic structure of the lyrics, which I like a lot."[100]

In the show's finale, in which the Leading Player tries to persuade Pippin to go out in a blaze of glory in a flaming suicide, he instead chooses domesticity. In Hirson's script, when asked how he feels, Pippin replies "Trapped, but happy – which isn't too bad for a musical comedy." Fosse cut the words "but happy". Actor John Rubinstein, who played Pippin, felt the audience recoil, and in the published version the full line is re-instated. Scott Miller, artistic director of St. Louis' New Line Theatre says, "Because the word 'happy' carries extra baggage in the world of musical comedy in which so many shows must end 'happily ever after,' it is dangerous to use that word carelessly. So the debate rages on. Is Pippin really happy? Can you feel trapped and happy at the same time? Can he acquire that much wisdom and self-knowledge that quickly? It's a decision you have to make."[101] This point is now moot, however. In the late 1990s a fringe revival was staged at London's Bridewell Theatre in 1998 by director-choreographer Mitch Sebastian that presented an entirely new ending. In this version, Pippin's stepson Theo, alone on stage, begins to sing an a capella reprise of "Corner of the Sky", suggesting a renewed existential crisis and a new target for the Leading Player's machinations.[102] This ending is now part of the

[100] Ibid.

[101] *Miller, Scott, From Assassins to West Side Story. Heinemann.* Portsmouth, NH, 1996

[102] The author attended the same performance of this as Stephen Schwartz, and witnessed his reaction first hand.

licensed version, and was included in the 2013 Broadway revival.

"Whether *Pippin* would have succeeded without Bob, who can say?" says Schwartz. "If Hal Prince had directed it... I think the script would have been better because I think Bob undercut things in the script. But be that as it may, the show worked."[103] In 2013 it was revived on Broadway by director Diane Paulus (1966-). "The joyous warmth", wrote Jon Magaril in *Slant Magazine*, "jibes well with the earnest side of book writer Roger O. Hirson and composer-lyricist Stephen Schwartz's material... Paulus honors the sincerity of Pippin's search, while keeping the wit about it... Her way into the material stands in direct contrast to Fosse... [who had] wrested control from Stephen Schwartz... and stamped out even the scent of sentiment... Paulus shifts that dynamic in one fell swoop... The primal pull between the [Leading Player] and Pippin... is lost, but it gives him space to develop the relationships elsewhere and it enables many of the other performers to shine."[104]

Fosse certainly inspired loyalty among his performers, if not with his collaborators. Actor Roy Scheider (1932-2008) who played a character modelled on Fosse in the 1979 film *All That Jazz* says, "He's the only director I know who was really

[103] Carol de Giere, *Defying Gravity – The Creative Career of Stephen Schwartz from Godspell to Wicked*, Applause Theatre Books, New York, 2008, p. 99.
[104] Jon Magarill, "Clinb on Board: Pippin at the Music Box Theatre", *Slant Magazine*, 11 May 2013 www.slantmagazine.com/article/climb-on-board-Pippin-at-the-Music-Box-Theatre

conversant with actors in understanding how they develop a character, how they do their work, what their homework is like, what their fears are, what their pluses and minuses are, how to leave an actor alone when he's cooking and how to ride him when he needs to be pushed. In other words, he was a director who went to scene study classes at his studio, who had read Stanislavsky, who had been in acting classes, who was himself a performer, both in movies and on the stage. So you were working with someone who was very close to you as a creative performer, not just as a creative director."[105]

Harold Prince's Broadway productions as director include *Cabaret, Follies, A Little Night Music, Pacific Overtures, Evita, Phantom of the Opera* and *Kiss of the Spider Woman.* Author Keith Garebian says, "His productions never abandon the performance impulse even as they refuse to be superficial or to dilute the serious or disturbing elements that push the form into new thematic territory."[106]

The musical *Cabaret* is an opportunity to compare Prince and Fosse's approaches directly, since Prince directed the 1966 Broadway production while Fosse made the 1971 film version. The musical began its journey as a very different show from the one it ended up as. English composer Sandy Wilson (1924-2014), creator of *The Boy Friend*, had been engaged by

---

[105] "Scene Specific Commentary for Roy Scheider", *All That Jazz* DVD, 20th Century Fox Home Video, F1-SGB 01095DVD
[106] Keith Garebian, *The Making of Cabaret*, Oxford University Press, New York, 2011, p 17.

producer David Black to adapt John Van Druten (1901-57)'s play *I Am a Camera* into a musical that was to be called *Goodbye to Berlin*. When Black's option on the material ran out, it was picked up by Prince, who hired Joe Masteroff (1919-) to write a new book. Prince then invited Wilson to play the score for Masteroff. "There was nothing wrong with the songs", says Masteroff, "except they all sounded like *The Boy Friend*. The fact that it was 1920s Berlin had led Wilson to do the same thing as he had for 1920s Brighton (or wherever it was)."[107] Prince eventually discarded Wilson's songs, feeling that he had trivialised the material. He hired John Kander (1927-) and Fred Ebb (1928-2004) to write a new score, and had Masteroff create a new character not found in either the Van Druten play or the Christoper Isherwood (1904-86) stories on which it was based. Masteroff also came up with the new title, *Cabaret*.

Prince felt there was something lacking. Then he recalled his Army experience in post-war occupied Germany. "The war was just over," says Prince, "so everything was just demolished in Germany, and yet there were opera houses still functioning, ballet companies still working. There was theatre. I was outside of Stuttgart and I hung out in a little bar called Maxim's which was in a bombed-out church. There was a little guy – an MC – with lots of makeup and eye-shadow and there were three huge Valkyrie ladies in diaphanous gowns galumphing around, and you'd have a couple of drinks and watch him trying to get a small audience into it, enthusiastic, and he

---

[107] Garebian, p.16.

was very obsequious and hard working, sweat a lot. Years later, 1966, we hadn't quite figured out how to do *Cabaret*. We'd done a version, and I thought it's not exciting enough. I drew on that guy and brought a friend in, Joel Grey, and introduced him to Kander and Ebb and they wrote for him, and that was the MC."[108]

Prince also hired set designer Boris Aronson (1898-1980), who had also designed the set for Van Druten's play. Aronson had grown up in Moscow under the influence of Vsevelod Meyerhold (1874-1940) and Alexander Tairov (1885-1950), and had embraced their sense of modernism. While he was thinking about *Cabaret* in 1965, Prince travelled to Moscow, where he saw a performance by the Taganka Theatre, which was heavily influenced by Meyerhold. He wanted to find a way to incorporate an element of surprise into what was fairly familiar material. Here, with help from Aronson, he found it. "There were technical devices which knocked me out. An apron built over the orchestra pit into which searchlights were sunk. These lights, slanted over the heads of the audience to the last row of the balcony, when lighted, instead of blinding, became a curtain of light behind which the scenery was changed. Paintings on the wall spoke, inanimate objects animated, disembodied hands, feet, and faces washed across the stage. There were puppets and projections, front and rear, and the source and colors of light were always a surprise...

---

[108] Steve Exeter, interview with Harold Prince, https://www.youtube.com/watch?v=UJXOWoB3ljo retrieved 21 November 2015.

Each of these ideas capitalized on the special relationships of live actors and live observers... And properly appreciated, it gives us the chance to string unseen emotional bands between actor and audience."[109]

The collaborators worked hard to evoke the atmosphere of an authentic Weimar Kabarett. Some people clearly didn't get this. Veteran Broadway conductor Lehman Engel – founder of the BMI Musical Theatre Workshops says, "I cannot understand why so much of *Cabaret* sounded like Kurt Weill... In the end, this sort of thing must fail since at best it is only an imitation." [110] Yet Vincent Patterson, the American director who mounted a revival of *Cabaret* in Berlin in 2006 says, "I am really blown away that Kander and Ebb and Joe Masteroff, who wrote the book, had not come to Berlin before they wrote this piece. They did this while sitting in New York... Somehow the muses got inside of them and informed them of not only the story that was so powerful, but the sentiment and the sounds of the music and the dialogue and the way people spoke and the feeling of this time."[111] Kander had immersed himself in the music of not only Kurt Weill (1900-50) who never actually wrote cabaret music, but of Friedrich Holländer (1896-1976), Mischa Spoliansky (1898-1985) and others of that period. Of course, it *is* an imitation – albeit a particularly skilful (and

[109] Harold Prince, *Contradictions: Notes on Twenty-six Years in the Theatre*, Dodd Mead, New York, 1974, p.93

[110] Lehman Engel, *Words with Music*, Schirmer Books, New York, 1972, p. 131.

[111] *Blue Angels and Pirate Jennys*, BBC Radio 4, 25 February 2006.

appropriate) one. (Engel later conceded that "*Cabaret* is a far better show than I had at first thought".[112])

"What I remember most", says Kander, "is that for months Hal and Joe Masteroff and [Ebb] and I would sit in a room and play a game that I called 'What if?' The director, writers, and composer sit in a room together and imagine the characters and elements of the story. That's an area where Hal's strength as a leader of collaboration shone through. We were inventing incidents that were going to be a part of the story. What if such and such happens? What if somebody throws a brick through the window?"[113]

When the film of *Cabaret* was made, Bob Fosse was hired to direct. "Today I get very antsy watching musicals in which people are singing as they walk down the street or hang out the laundry," he told *New York* magazine in 1974. "In fact, I think it looks a little silly. You can do it on stage. The theatre has its own personality – it conveys a removed reality. The movies bring that reality closer."[114] Masteroff's script was mostly discarded, except for the MC's part, played again by Joel Grey. The new script by Jay Presson Allen (1922-2006) returned to the Van Druten play and the Isherwood stories. Allen, whose work would be revised by "research consultant" Hugh Wheeler (1912-87), found Fosse "so depressed that it

[112] Engel, ibid, p.263.

[113] Kander, Ebb & Lawrence, pp. 40-1.

[114] Paul Gardner, "Bob Fosse Off His Toes", *New York* Magazine, 16 December 1974, Cited in Michael B. Druxman, *The Musical from Broadway to Hollywood*, A.S. Barnes and Company, New York, 1980, p. 143

took two hours just to get him in the frame of mind for work."[115] Only the diagetic songs were retained, supplemented by several new Kander and Ebb songs (Jerome Robbins had urged Prince to eliminate the "book" songs from the stage version). With the exception of "Tomorrow Belongs to Me", all were sung in the cabaret by either Sally Bowles or the M.C.

While the stage production focused on Frau Schneider, who was played on Broadway by Lotte Lenya (1898-1981), the film restored the basic plot line of *I Am a Camera*, shifting the focus back to Sally Bowles, a singer at a night club (called the Lady Windermere in Van Druten's play; this became the Kit Kat Klub in the musical). Isherwood had based his original Sally Bowles on a real-life English singer named Jean Ross (1911-73) who had performed in the chorus in Max Reinhardt's production of *Tales of Hoffmann*. (In the film, Sally – played by Liza Minelli – dreams of being cast in a Max Reinhardt show.)

"When the movie was made with Liza," says Prince, "I thought it was a terrific movie but I thought Liza was too talented for it. I've always thought that. The girl should not be the central, huge musical theatre talent. The girl is an irresponsible breath of life and a good character, but the show is about the rise of the National Socialist party in Germany... and we made a hit out of it."[116] However, you could make the same

[115] *Martin Gottfried, All His Jazz: The Life & Death Of Bob Fosse.: Da Capo Press, New York* Gottfried. p.205.
[116] https://www.youtube.com/watch?v=a8Fgho216k8 (C) 2012 Sony Music Entertainment accessed 22 November 2015.

argument about Joel Grey's MC. It would seem natural that Fosse would be unlikely to resist adding a bit of show business pizzazz, but in this case, I would argue that he was right. Minelli had been Kander and Ebb's original choice, vetoed by Prince. However, it's possible that casting a weak singer – Jill Haworth (1945-2011) in the Broadway production – was taking realism a bit too far. We accept that Sally Bowles is a tragically flawed underachiever. Fosse gave the audience a satisfying performance while still scoring a point or two against the Nazis.

Of Prince's collaborations with Stephen Sondheim, all but two of the ideas originated with Prince. (The exceptions were *Follies* (1971) and *Sweeney Todd* (1979).) *Company* (1970) is often described as Broadway's first "concept" musical, although you could argue that the notion really began with *Cabaret*. Professor Stephen Banfield says, "Inasmuch as it marked the start of the partnership with Harold Prince as director... and with Michael Bennett as choreographer and Boris Aronson as set designer, *Company* fits this definition well enough, as it does its extension whereby the director decides what the play is 'about' and seeks to have this reflected or stated in all the disciplines and elements of production."[117]

Company began as eleven one-act plays about marriage by actor George Furth (1932-2008). The plan was for Kim Stanley to play a different wife in each of the eleven plays. Unable to raise the money, Furth

---

[117] Stephen Banfield, *Sondheim's Broadway Musicals*, University of Michigan Press, Ann Arbor, MI, 1993, p. 147.

turned to his friend Sondheim who, in turn, referred it to Prince. It was Prince who saw it as a musical, with one central, unmarried character observing the marriages of his friends.

In the end, only two of Furth's plays – the "karate" couple and the pot-smoking couple – were used, and he wrote three more. "To George and me", writes Sondheim, "the problem of merging unrelated scenes into a unified evening seemed an impossible one to solve (making the project irresistible) until we came up with the now obvious solution – to turn the different outsiders into a single person. We called him Robert, known to his friends as Bob, Bobby, Robby and Rob-o, and soon the central theme of the evening emerged; the challenge of maintaining relationships in a society becoming increasingly depersonalized."[118]

As Sondheim often says, content dictated form. Although neither he nor Prince is fans of Berthold Brecht, "All the songs had to be used, I'm sorry to say, in a Brechtian way as comment and counterpoint."[119]

Prince also sometimes imposed his vision on other people's projects, although not in quite as heavy-handed or confrontational a manner as Fosse. While in London working on the West End production of *A Little Night Music*, Sondheim chanced to see the

---

[118] Stephen Sondheim, *Finishing the Hat*, Virgin Books, London, 2010, p. 165

[119] Craig Zadan, *Sondheim & Co.*, Da Capo Press, New York, 1974, p. 117

melodrama *Sweeney Todd* by English playwright
Christopher Bond (1945-) at Theatre Royal Stratford
East. Bond's version combined the traditional
Victorian pot-boiler with elements of Alexandre
Dumas's *The Count of Monte Cristo*. Sondheim was
determined to make it into a musical, and brought it
to Prince.

"*Sweeney [Todd}* was very much Steve's show. I didn't
get it. I got it as I went along. It's about revenge, and
I don't think I'm a vengeful guy. I don't think I feel
revenge. I recognise its existence. The idea of it
drains me. It hurts my energy level. But I got into it
because it's very possible I imposed something on it...
I wanted it to have some social significance. The story
takes place during the beginning of the industrial age
in England and that all of these people obviously turn
to cannibalism. Some of them don't even know that
they're inadvertently cannibals, but basically I
thought they're all sharing one thing. They never
breathe clean air, they never see sunlight. From the
day they're born to the day they die, they're victims.
And so I said to [designer] Eugene Lee, 'Let's do it in
a factory, and let's put a glass roof on it that makes it
claustrophobic and let's tell all of these people that
they're in the same spot , really, as the two leading
characters in the play. They're all victims of the
industrial age. This was a time when kids were on
the assembly line for fourteen hours a day doing
piecework and so on. That pulled the whole show
together for me."[120] He responded by having scenic
designer Eugene Lee (1939-) build a huge 19th

---

[120] Exeter, op. cit.

century factory on stage, suggesting a sort of Dickensian evocation of the industrial revolution. "The sense of the city," says Sondheim, "which is, in fact, a sense of the industrial revolution, machinery, steel, and all that, is very much Hal's approach to the material."[121]

While Prince and Sondheim may not have entirely agreed on the scale of the show – Sondheim wanted a chamber piece, whereas Prince felt the Grand Guignol aspect demanded something larger – they were still broadly on the same page. Prince may have imposed certain aspects of his vision on the show, but – unlike Fosse on *Pippin* – he did not try to obliterate the original authors' vision. He did, however, once sign on to a project that he later tried to get out of: *Baker Street* (1965).

Producer Alexander Cohen (1920-2000) had originally signed to produce a musical version of the Sherlock Holmes stories with a book by Jerome Coopersmith (1925-) but with a score by unknown writers that was unworkable. Cohen then brought in Raymond Jessel (1929-2015) and Marian Grudeff (1927-2006), who were veterans of the long running Canadian satirical revue *Spring Thaw* to, at first augment, and ultimately to replace the score. Their original director was to be Michael Langham (1919-2011), who was then Artistic Director of the Stratford Festival. He then became unavailable, and was replaced by Broadway veteran Joshua Logan (1908-88). "We got along famously with him", says Jessel, "but he had one of his manic

---

[121] Daniel Gerould, *Melodrama*, New York Literary Forum, 1980, P.11

episodes."[122] (Logan was bi-polar.) He was then replaced by Prince, who had just come off directing *She Loves Me*, and was looking to direct a show that he did not produce. "He didn't like all of our score from the get-go", says Jessel. "It is calamitous to accept inferior material," says Prince. "There are so many surprises in the making of a show, unanticipated disappointments, problems, you cannot afford to make compromises up front."[123] He wanted to replace Jessel and Grudeff with Sheldon Harnick and Jerry Bock, with whom he had done *She Loves Me* and *Fiddler on the Roof*, but Cohen stood by his existing team, and there was no time to find another director. Even so, Harnick and Bock wrote three of the songs, un-credited. *Baker Street* lasted for 311 performances.

"Preparation is getting everything you need to know of a sensory nature about the characters", says Prince. "Where the story's taking place – all those sorts of things – what things smell like, taste like, sound like and so on. That's an exercise you share with your designer as well. Boris Aronson taught me that years ago. He was the greatest designer who ever lived, I think. I never saw him pick up a pen and draw something and say, 'What do you think of this?' Instead, he'd say 'Let's talk about the food. Let's talk about what the restaurants were like. Let's talk about the sound on the street.' And so *Cabaret*, for one, was a black box with selective bits of scenery and one huge surprise. I looked at the model for the first time and there was this waffled, wobbly funhouse mirror

---

[122] Mel Atkey, *Broadway North: the Dream of a Canadian Musical Theatre*, Natural Heritage Books, Toronto, 2006, p. 118.
[123] Prince, P. 114.

angled at the audience, and they came in and sat down and could see this distorted view of themselves, and it's like saying 'that's your metaphor, folks'"

"I have two left feet," says Prince, "but my best work is characterised by movement, by how I will move a block of people you would call an ensemble or chorus, and they are moving the way dancers would move. It's just that their feet aren't doing anything, because I wouldn't know how to tell them that. Jerry [Robbins] moved people diagonally across a stage, from upstage down, directly downstage, turn around, move directly upstage. Strange energies come from all of that. The theatre that he entered and that I entered moved laterally. They'd drop a drop and things would move from left to right or right to left and they'd change scenery upstage. There'd be doors. I haven't had a door in a show for as long as I can remember. That whole world of inviting the audience to use its imagination and fill in the blank spaces is the difference between what I do and what people who do realistic films do. Films weren't always realistic. I love old black and white silent films. They were forced perspective and all kinds of strange, wonderful things that I use in the theatre. I'm a huge admirer of [Orson] Welles. It started with that Mercury Theatre production [of *Julius Caesar*]. I do think *Citizen Kane* is as nourishing to me, a theatre director, as anything I've ever done."[124]

---

[124] Exeter, op. cit.

This was originally written as an essay for my MA in Musical Theatre at Goldsmiths, 2016.

Bibliography

Banfield, Stephen, *Sondheim's Broadway Musicals*, University of Michigan Press, 1993.

Beddow, Margery, *Bob Fosse's Broadway*, Heinemann, Portsmouth, NH, 1996

Garebian, Keith, *The Making of Cabaret*, Oxford University Press, New York, 2011.

Gottfried, Martin, *All His Jazz – the Life and Death of Bob Fosse*, Da Capo Press, New York, 1998.

Hirsch, Foster, *Harold Prince and the American Musical Theatre*, Applause Theatre Books, New York, 2005.

Ilson, Carol, *Harold Prince – a Director's Journey*, Limelight Editions, New York, 2000

Lawrence, Greg with Kander, John and Ebb, Fred, *Colored Lights – Forty Years of Words and Music, Show Biz, Collaboration and All That Jazz*, Faber and Faber Inc., New York, 2003.

McWaters, Debra, *The Fosse Style*, University Press of Florida, Gaiesville, FL, 2008

Wasson, Sam, *Fosse*, Mariner Books, New York, 2013.

Mel Atkey

Author

Mel Atkey has written four other books, *When We Both Got to Heaven* and *Broadway North: The Dream of a Canadian Musical Theatre*, both published by Natural Heritage Books, and *A Million Miles from Broadway – Musical Theatre Beyond New York and London* and *Running Away with the Circus – or "Now is the Winter of our Missing Tent"*, published by Friendlysong. He has contributed articles to various magazines, newspapers (and one academic journal) in his native Canada. He has worked in radio and television as a broadcaster, but his first love is musical theatre, a subject on which he has lectured internationally. He was a finalist in the International Musical of the Year Competition in Aarhus, Denmark, in 1996, and has been short-listed for the *Vivian Ellis* and *Ken Hill Prizes*, the *Quest for New Musicals* and *Musical Stairs*. His first recorded song, "Far Away" received airplay on radio across Canada and the United States, and he has written music on commission for CBC Radio and for the 1989 Canada Day Celebrations in Vancouver. He made his New York debut in 2001 with the Off-Broadway musical *O Pioneers!* with book by Robert Sickinger. He and Sickinger's second collaboration, *A Little Princess*, opened in 2003. Mel Atkey is a writer associate of Mercury Musical Developments, and a member of the Writers' Union of Canada. He is now based in London, England.

Books by Mel Atkey:

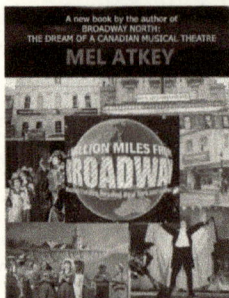

Musical theatre is – and always has been – an international form, not just an American one. It can take root anywhere. Such hit standards as "The Glow Worm", "Brazil", "Mack the Knife", "I Will Wait for You" and "El Condor Pasa" came from foreign language musicals. This book explores the work that exists outside of New York. Not the many franchised versions of *Fiddler on the Roof* and *Grease* that have played everywhere from Tel Aviv to Abu Dabi, but indigenous musical theatre created in places other than New York by people other than New Yorkers and drawing on traditions other than just those of Broadway.

296 Pages | Paperback | ISBN 9780991695706

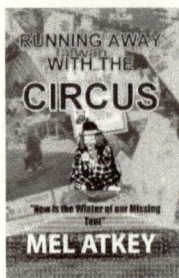

Running Away with the Circus (or, "Now is the Winter of our Missing Tent"

"If some clairvoyant had told me that I'd be spending my nights in a shipping container in Taiwan, guarding seven tigers, six Chihuahuas, five bears, four sea lions, three geese, two horses and a 'killer dog' named Ludwig, I'd have said 'You're supposed to read the tea leaves, not smoke them.'" -- Mel Atkey

ISBN 9780991695713

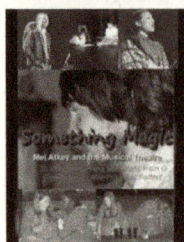

Something Magic A Collection of songs from musicals written by Mel Atkey. Mr. Atkey has been writing musicals ever since he was in high school in his native Vancouver. He was a finalist for the Musical of the Year competition in Aarhus, Denmark, and his work has been short-listed for the Vivian Ellis Prize, the Quest for New Musicals, the Ken Hill Prize and Musical Stairs. His two-character musical Perfect Timing was a finalist in the 1996 Musical of the Year competition in Aarhus, Denmark, and was showcased at Greenwich Theatre, London, in 2005. He made his New York debut in 2001 with O Pioneers, and followed it in 2003 with A Little Princess, both with book by Robert Sickinger.

ISBN 978-0-9916957-2-0
Friendlysong Books, Order from Lulu.com